EXOTIC SPIDERS COLORING BOOK
By Valeriia Laryoshyna

First paperback edition May 2023

Book design by Valeriia Laryoshyna

ISBN: 9798394355059

Published by Kindle Direct Publishing

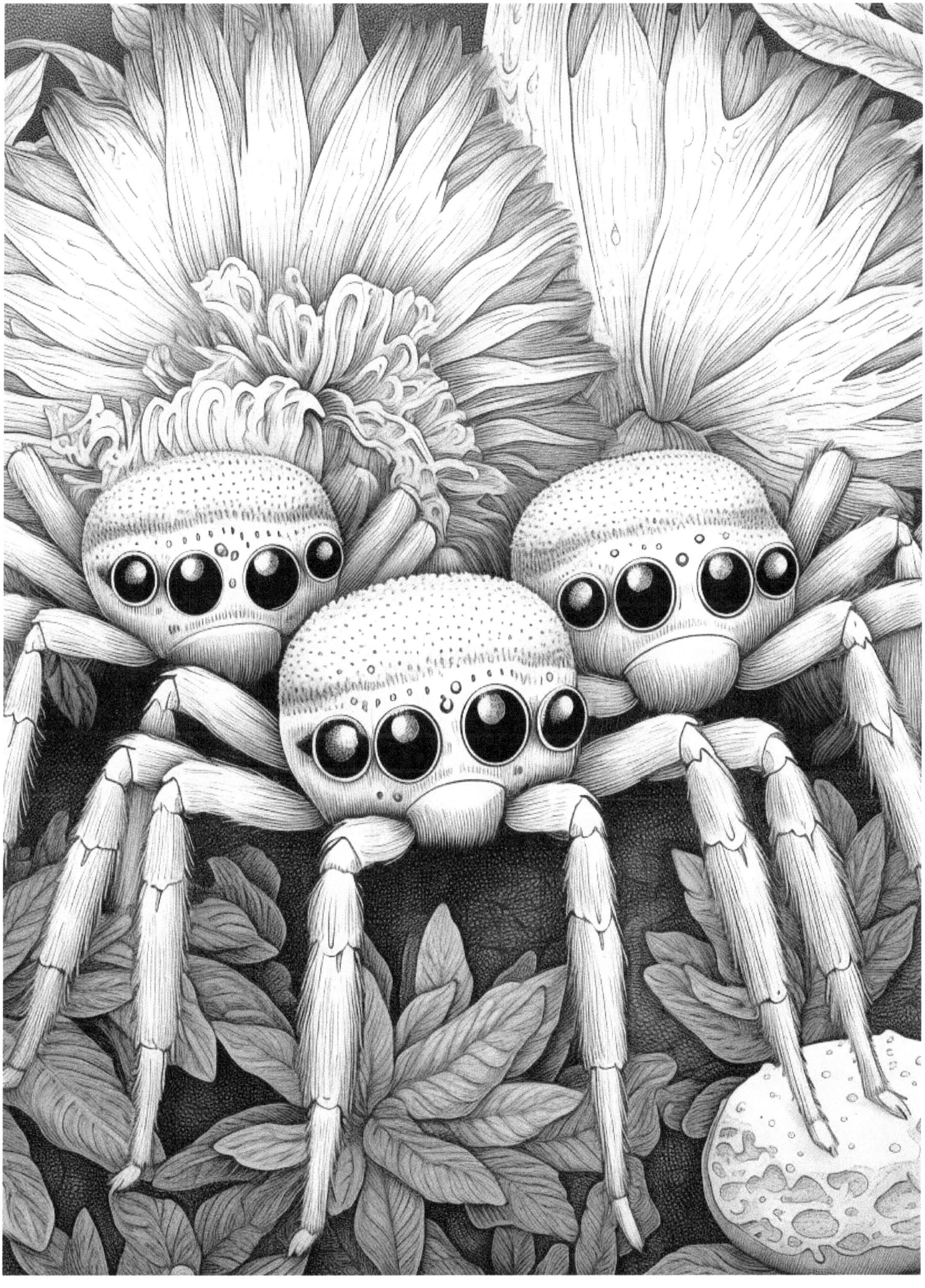

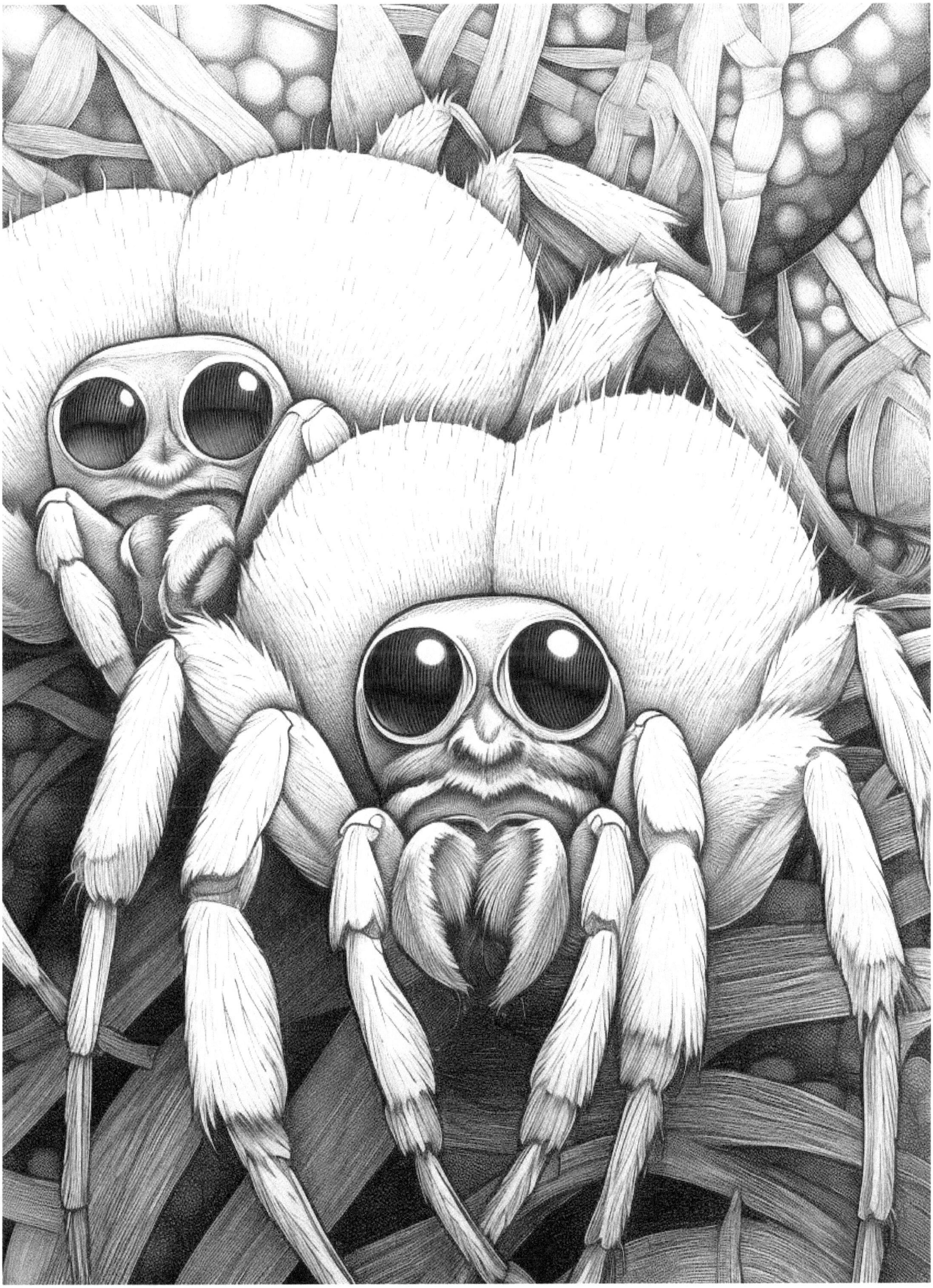

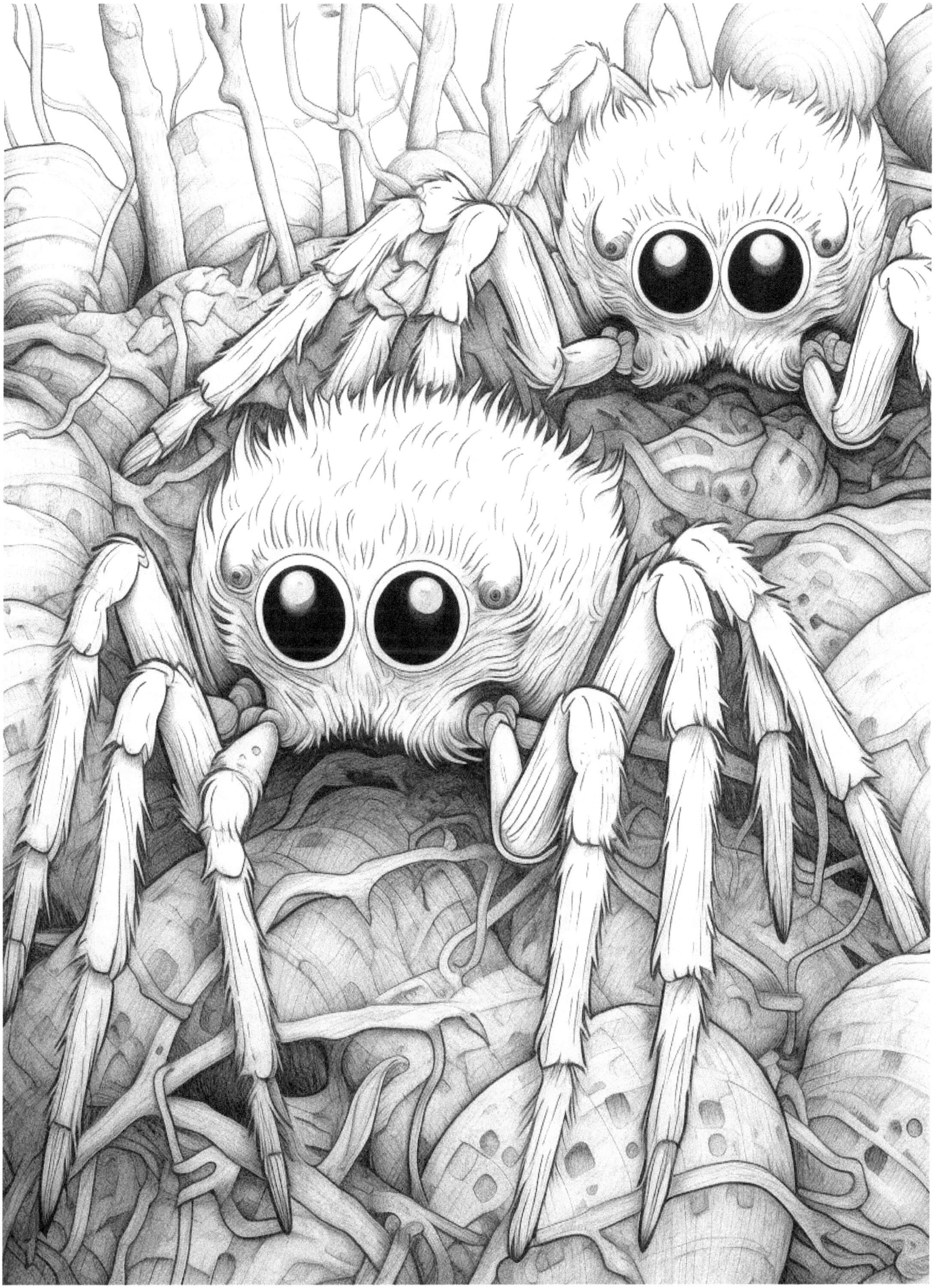

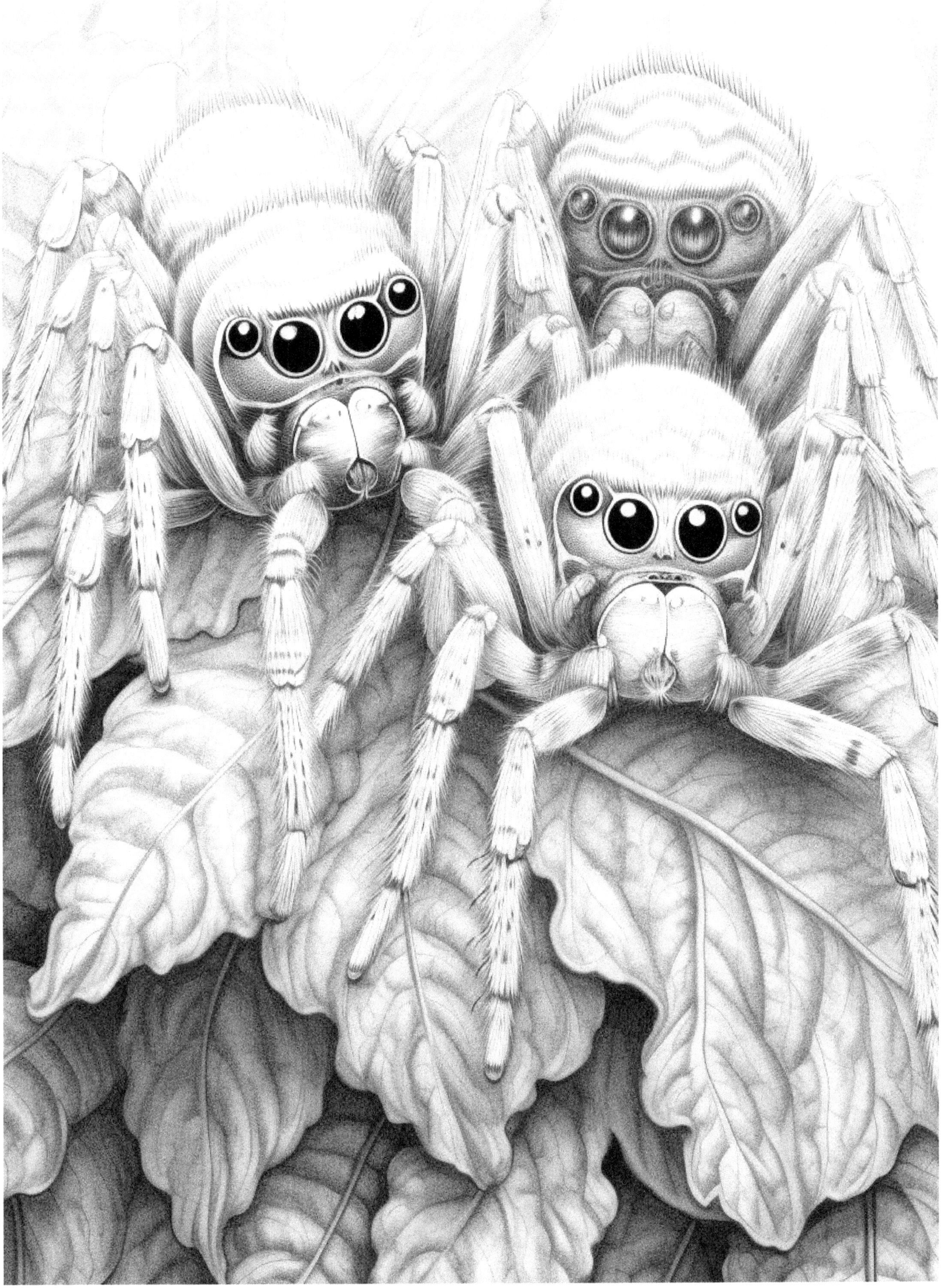

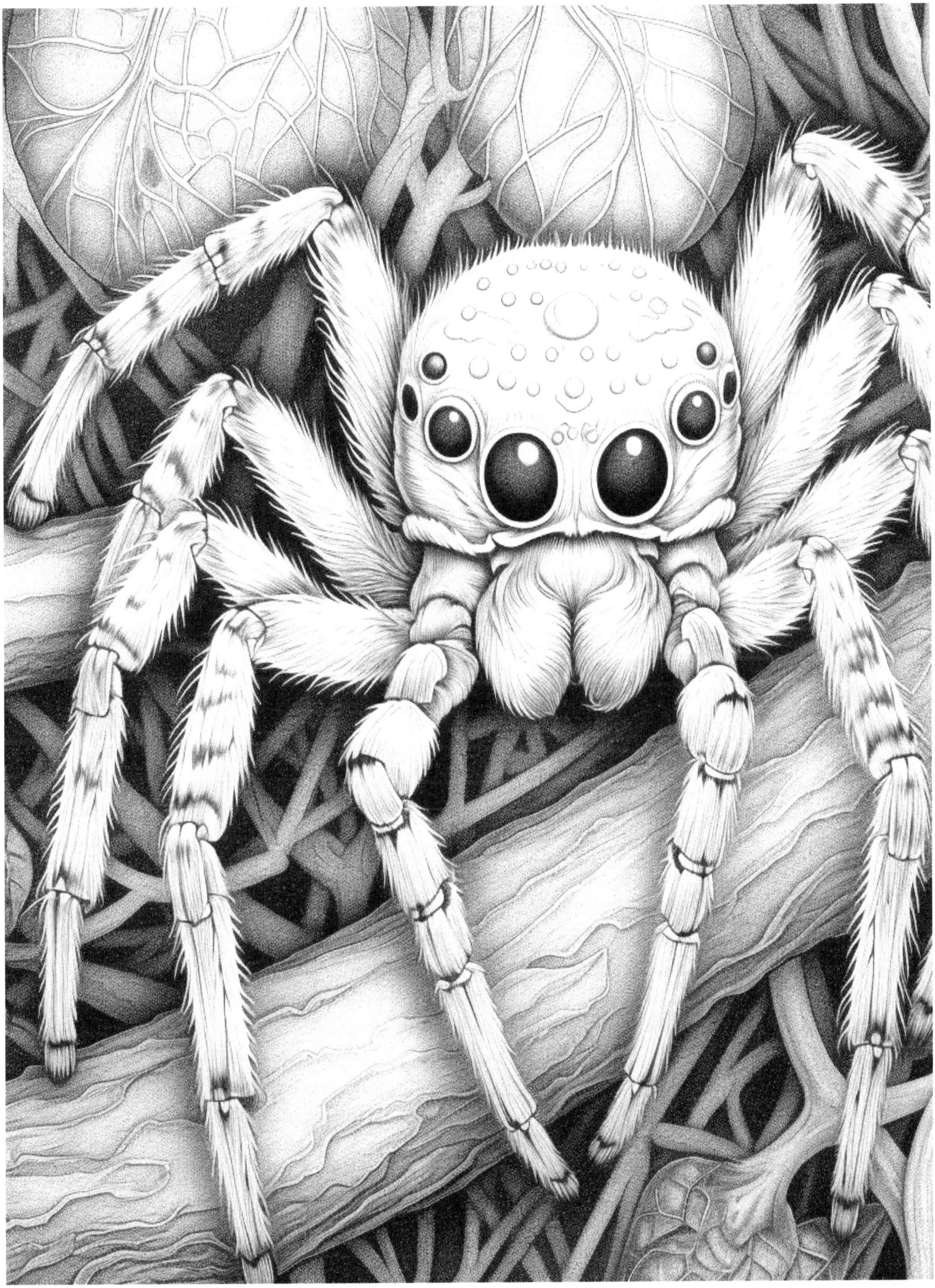

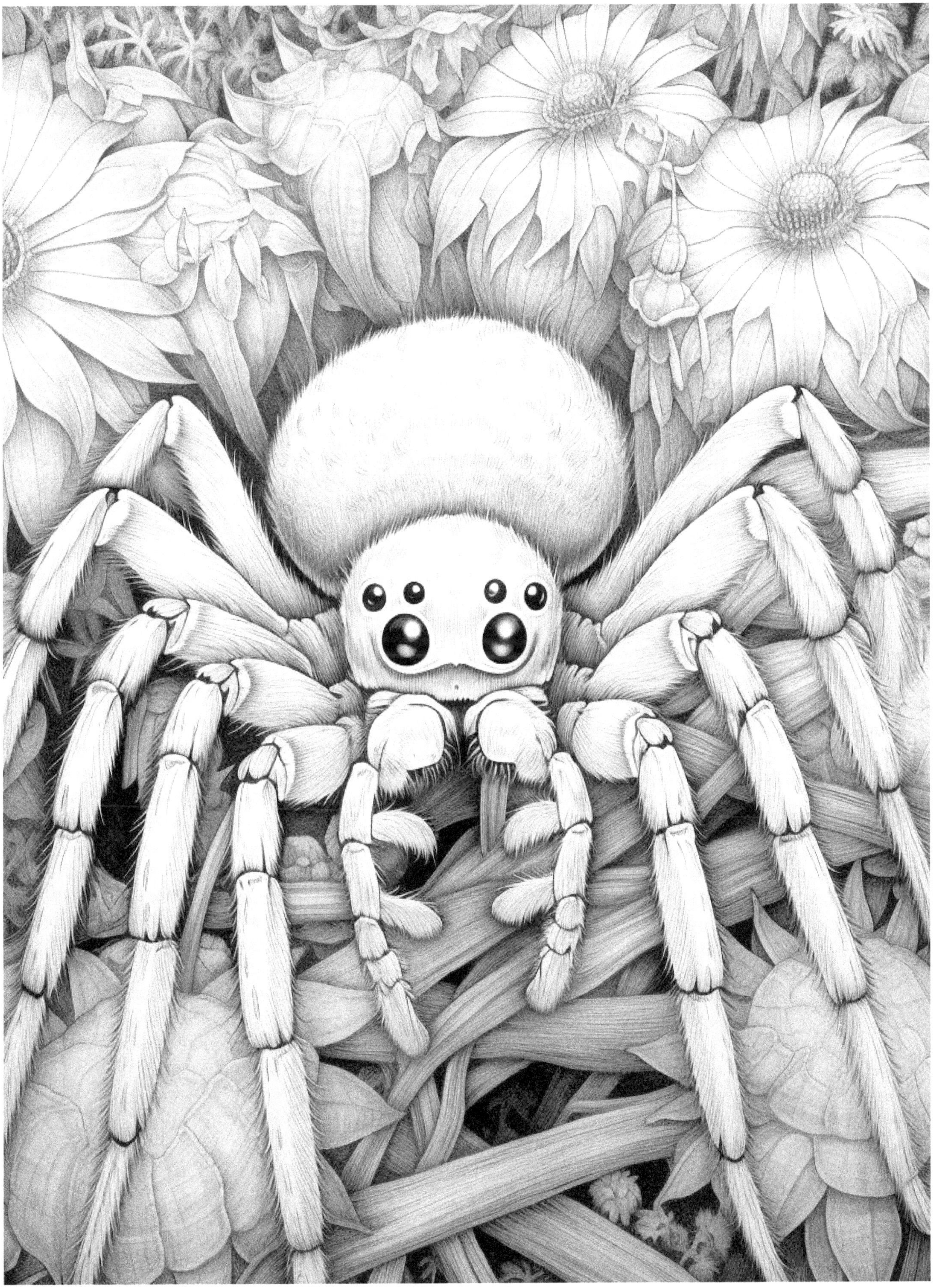

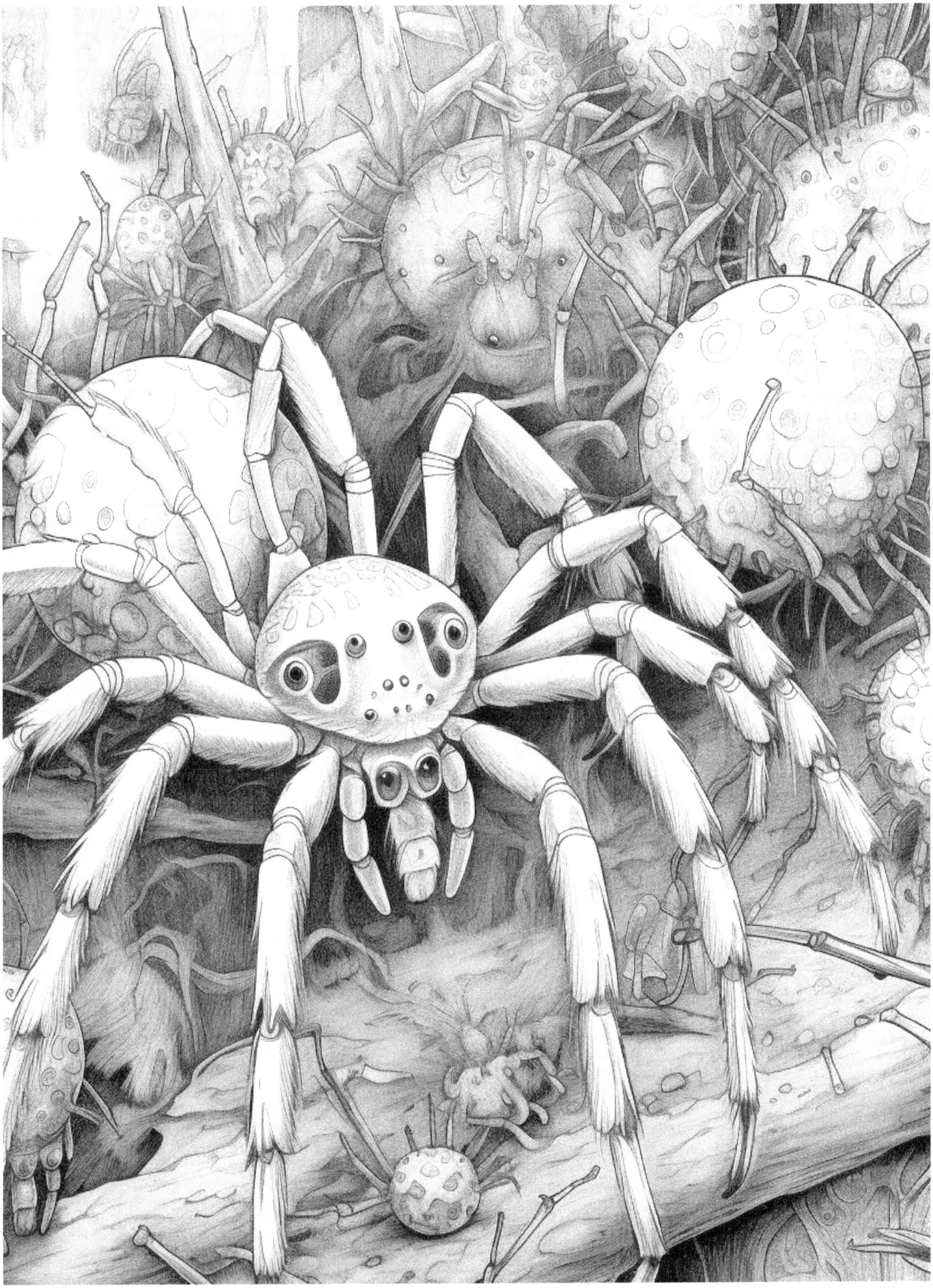

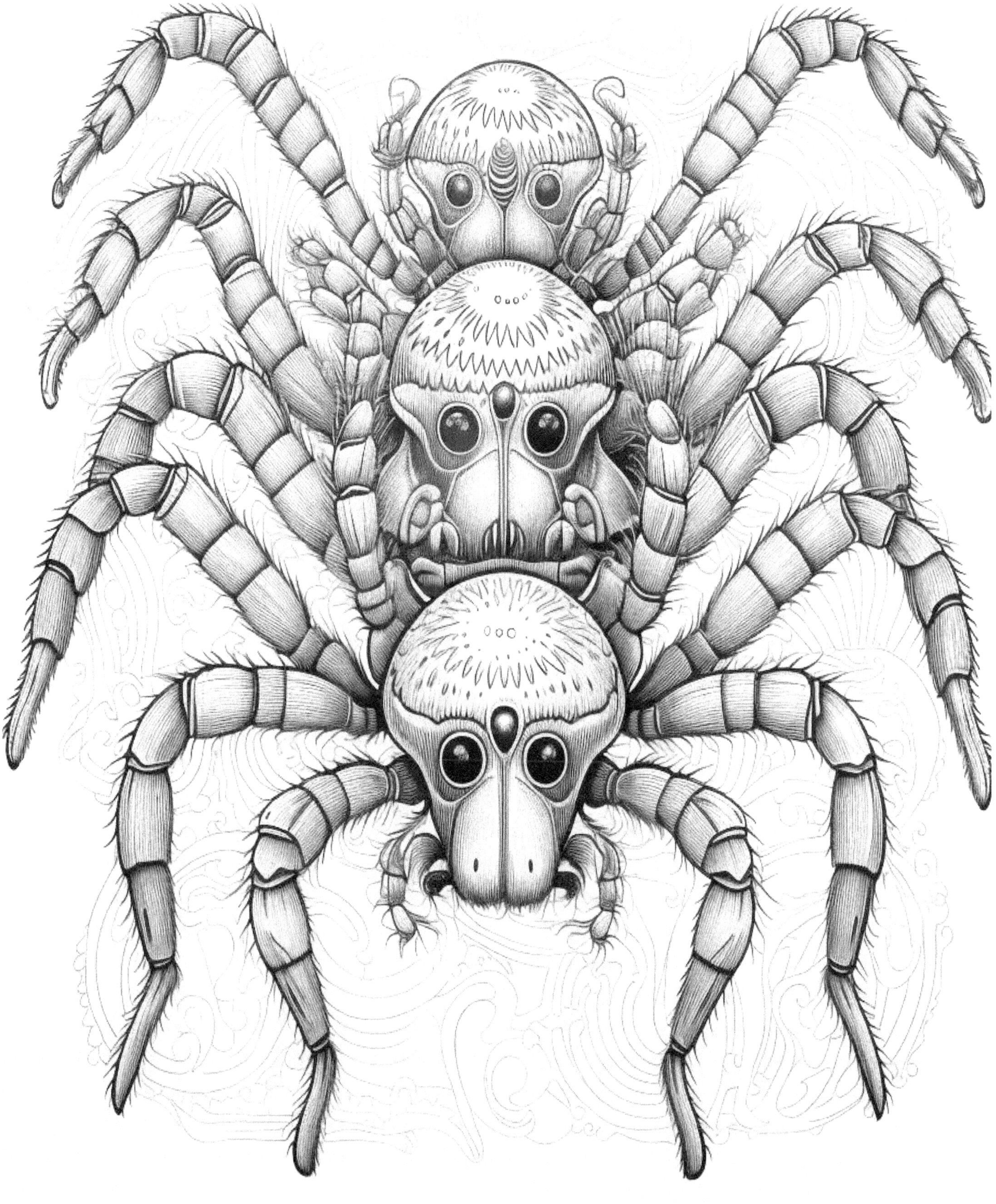

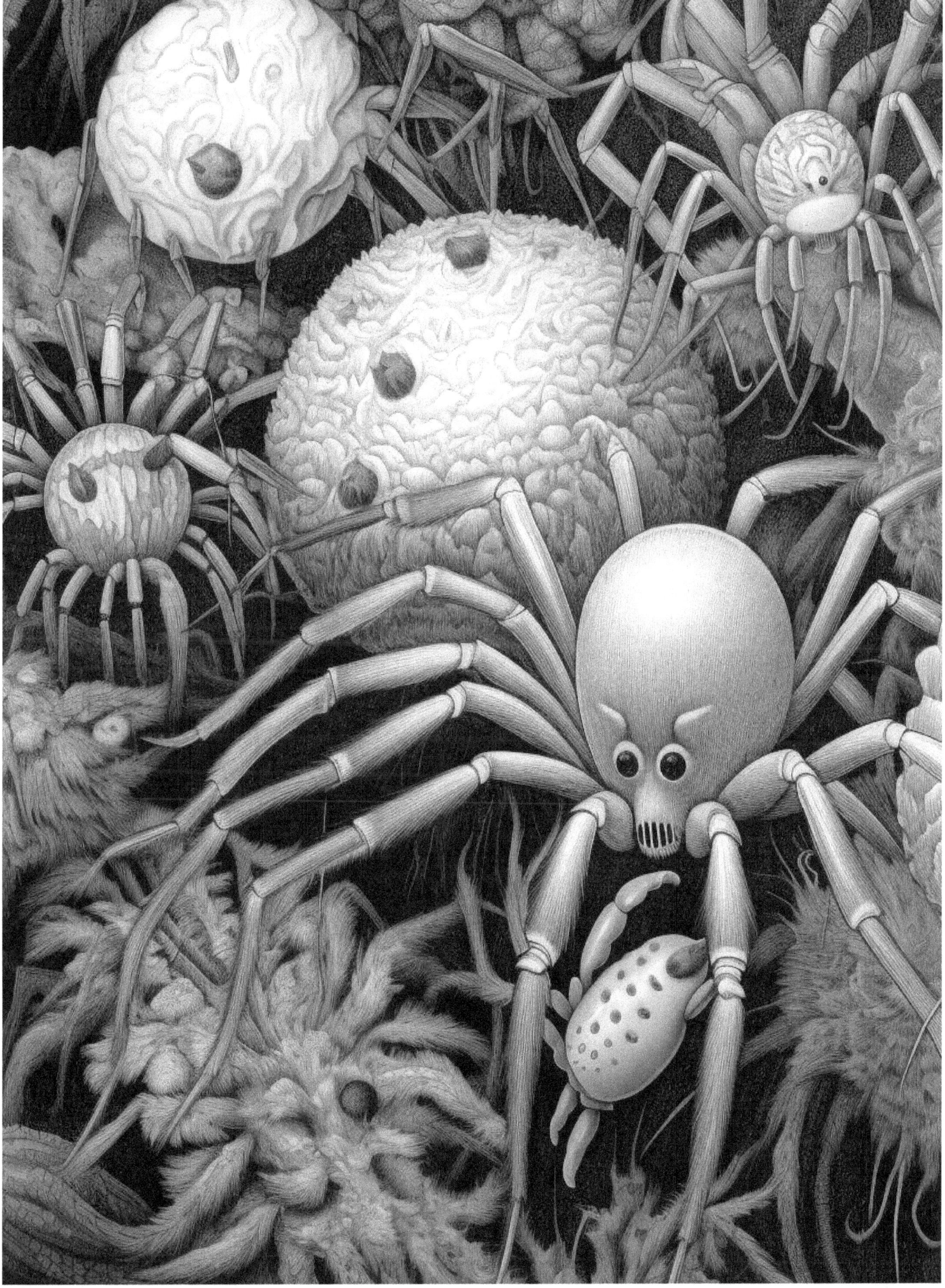

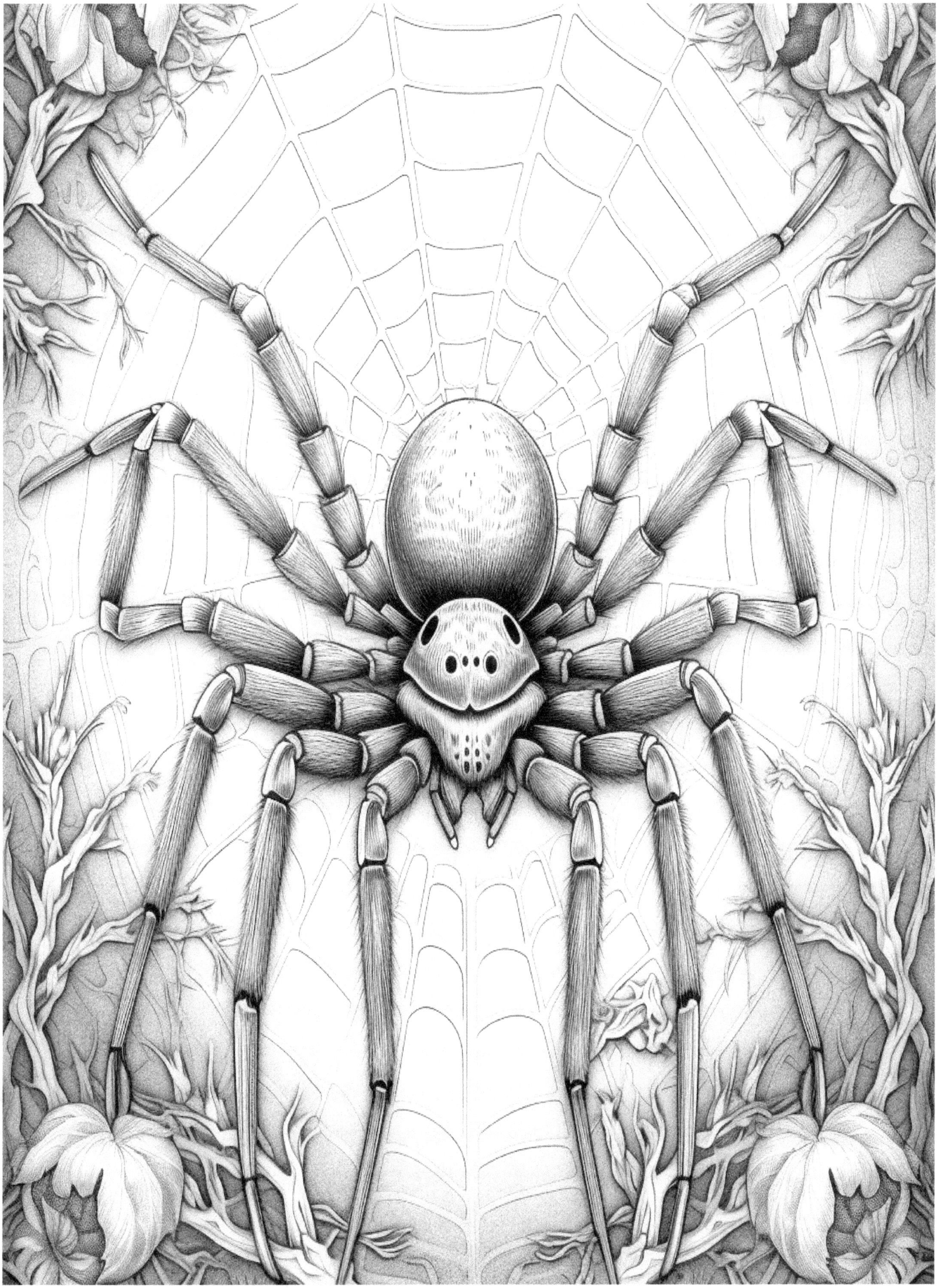

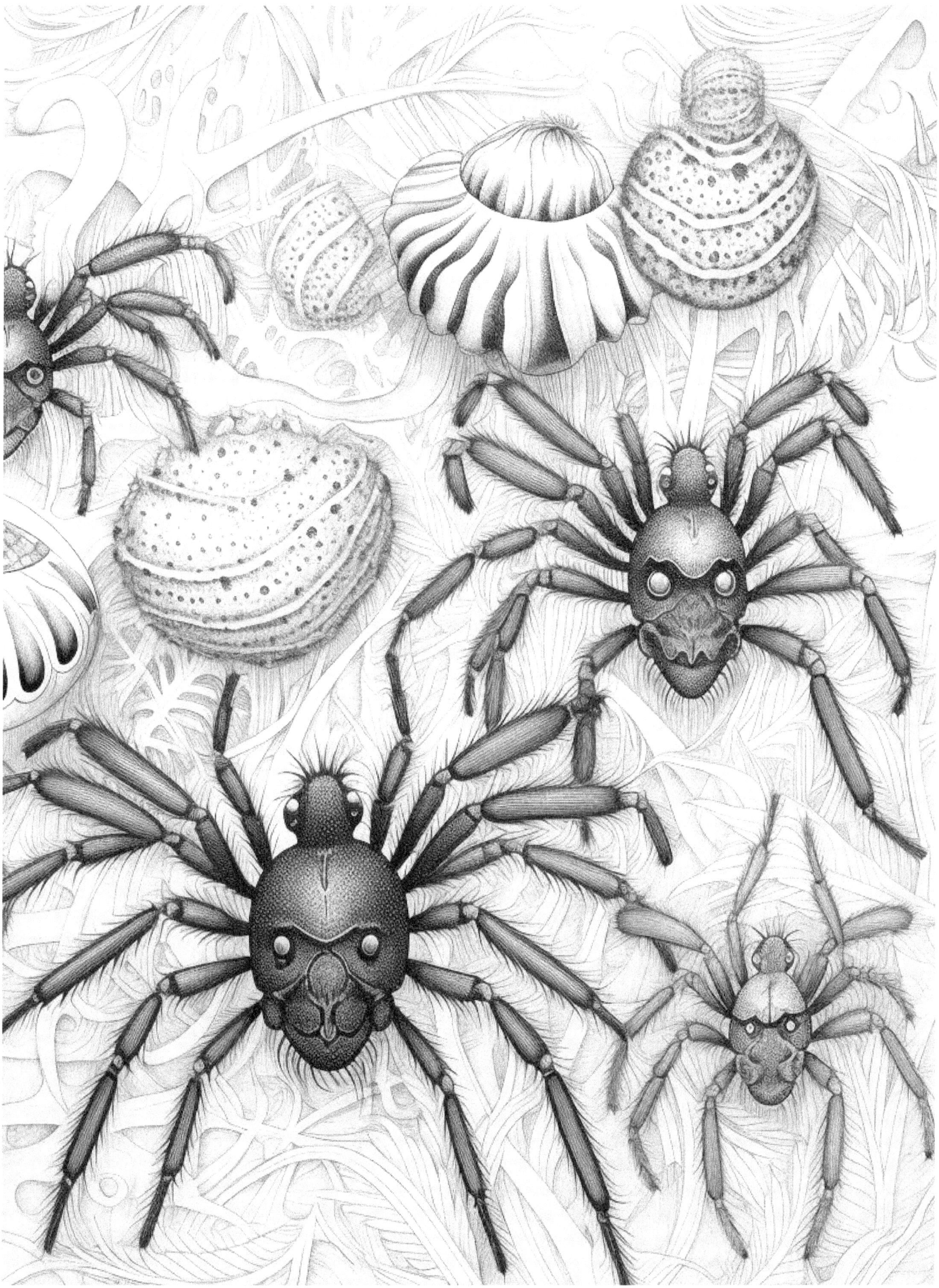

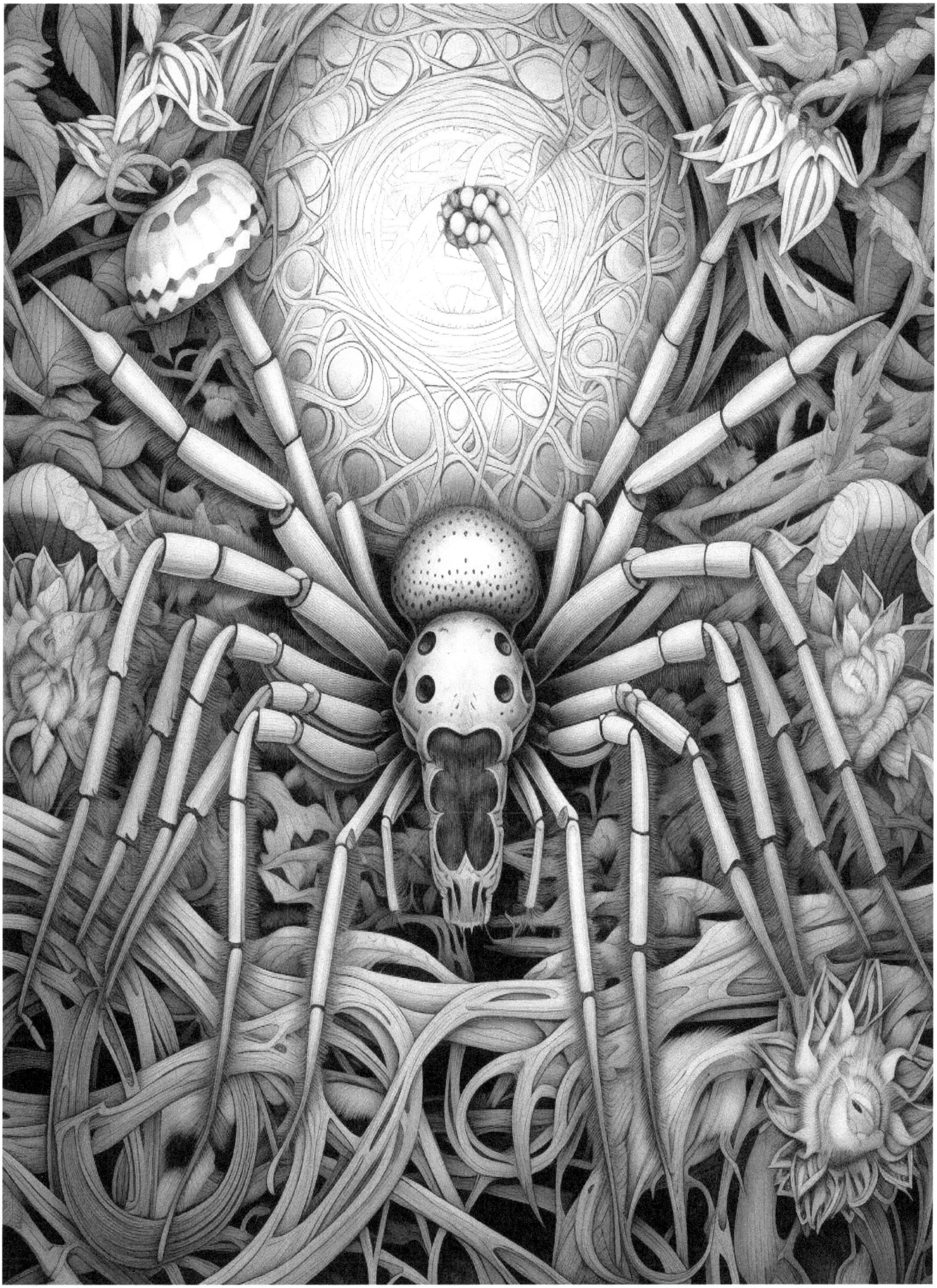

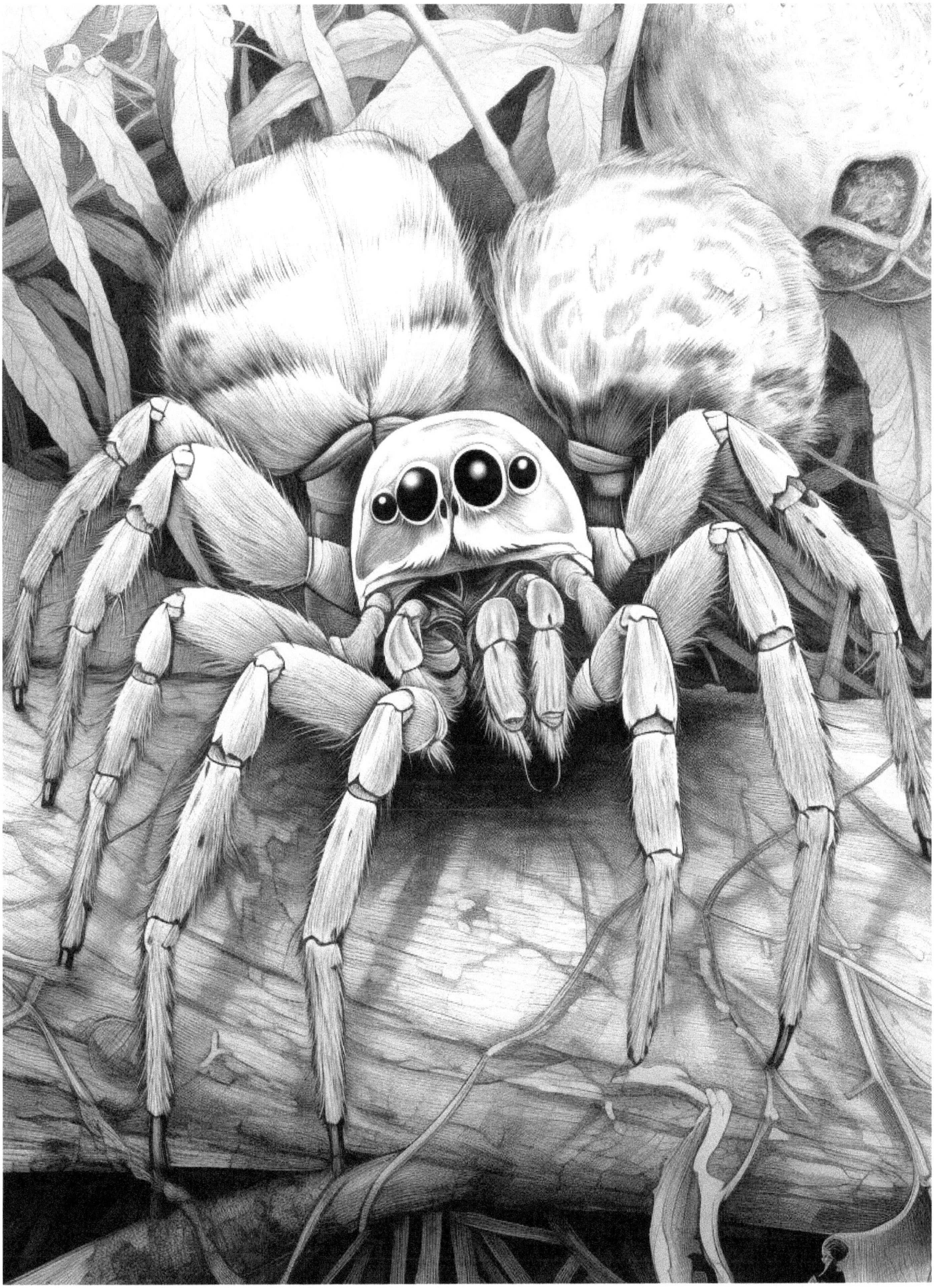

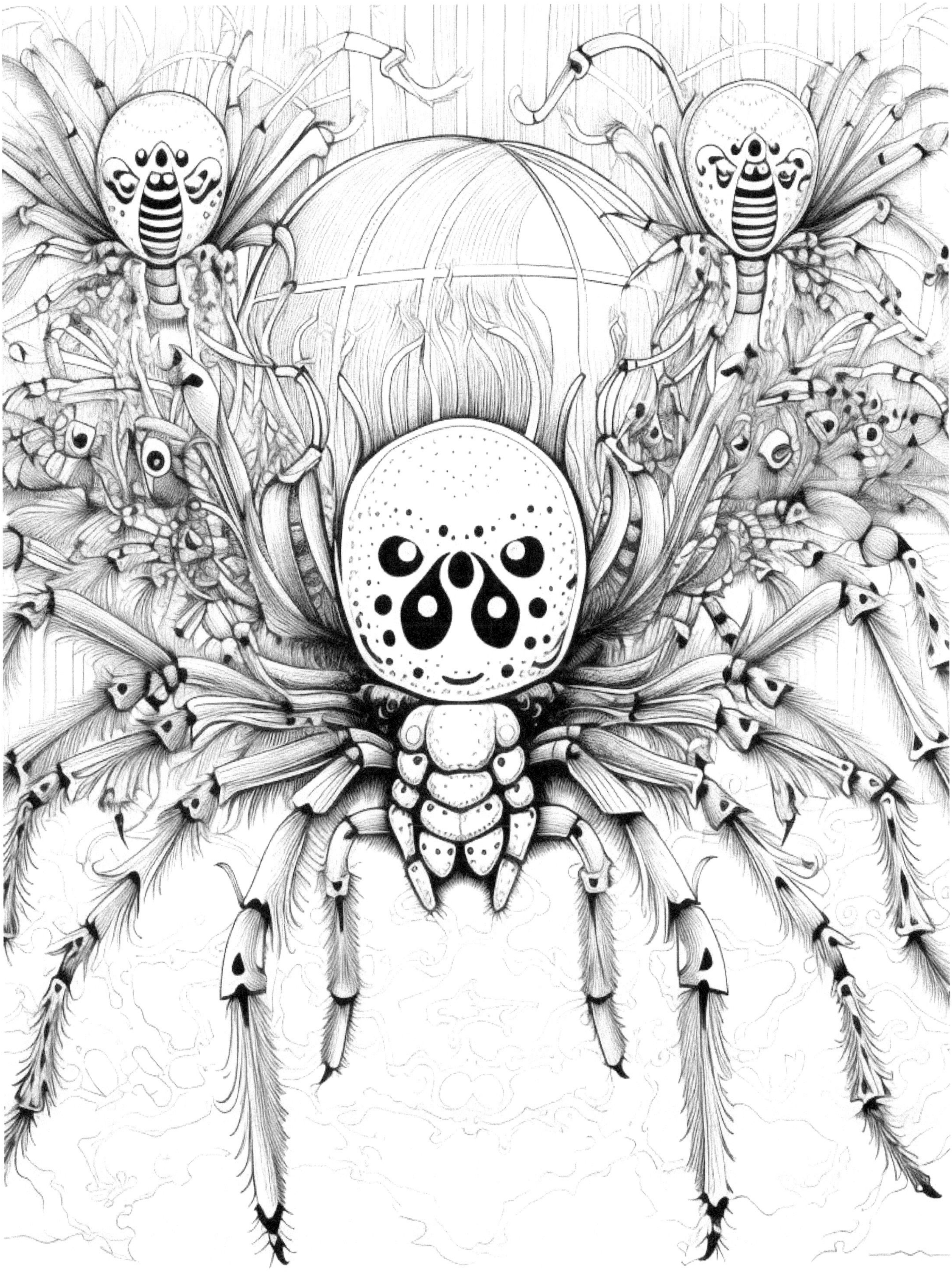

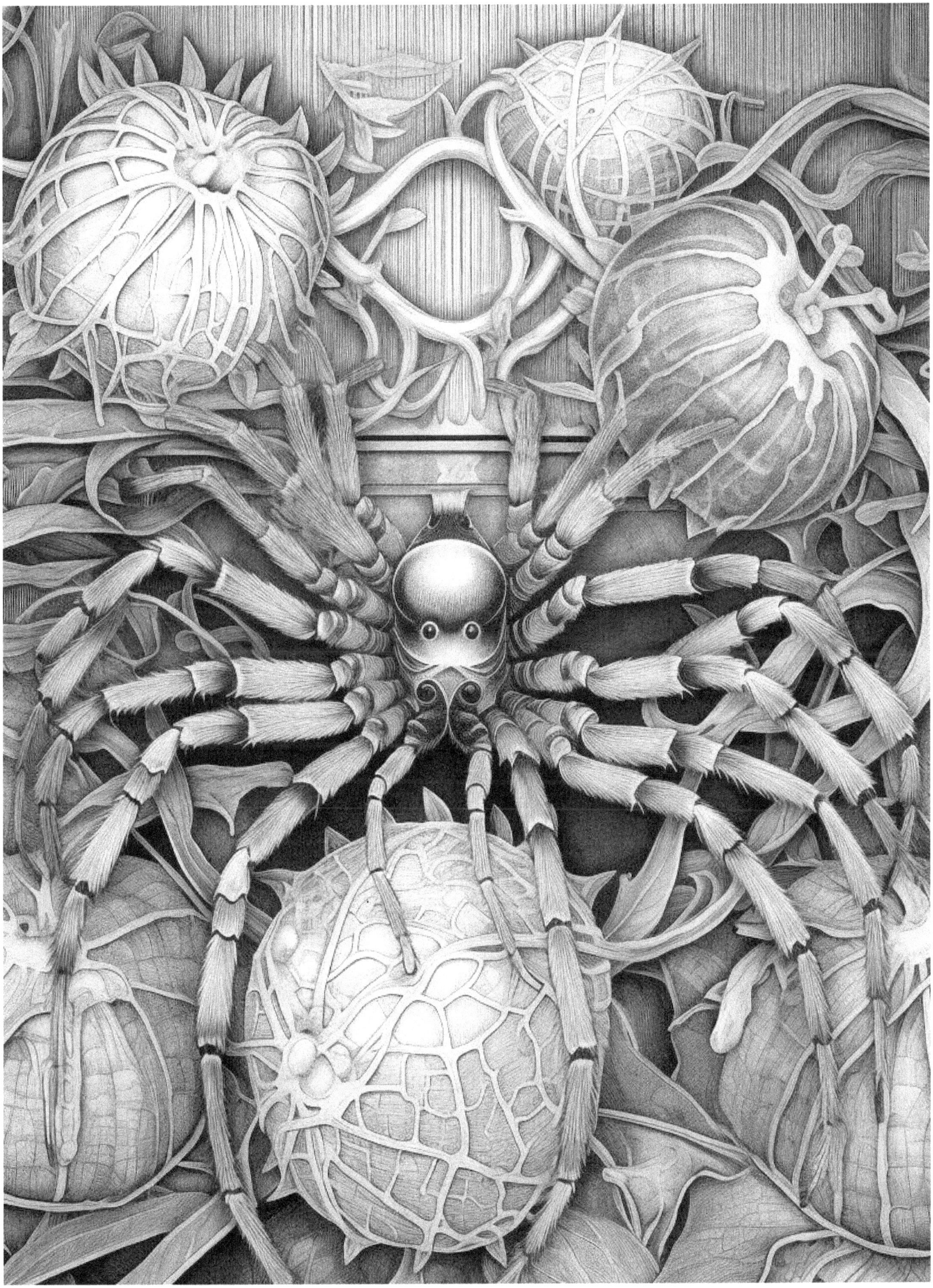

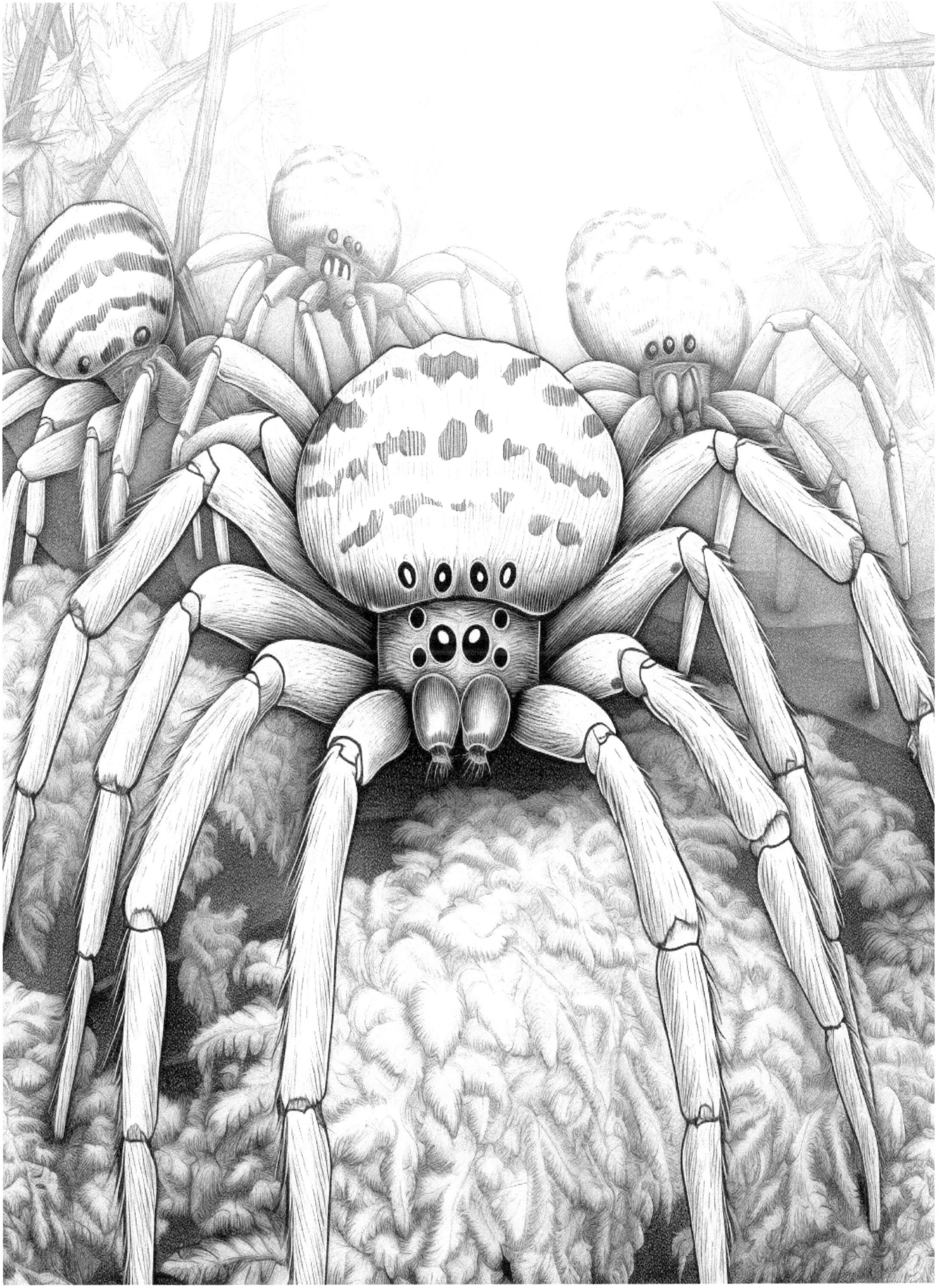

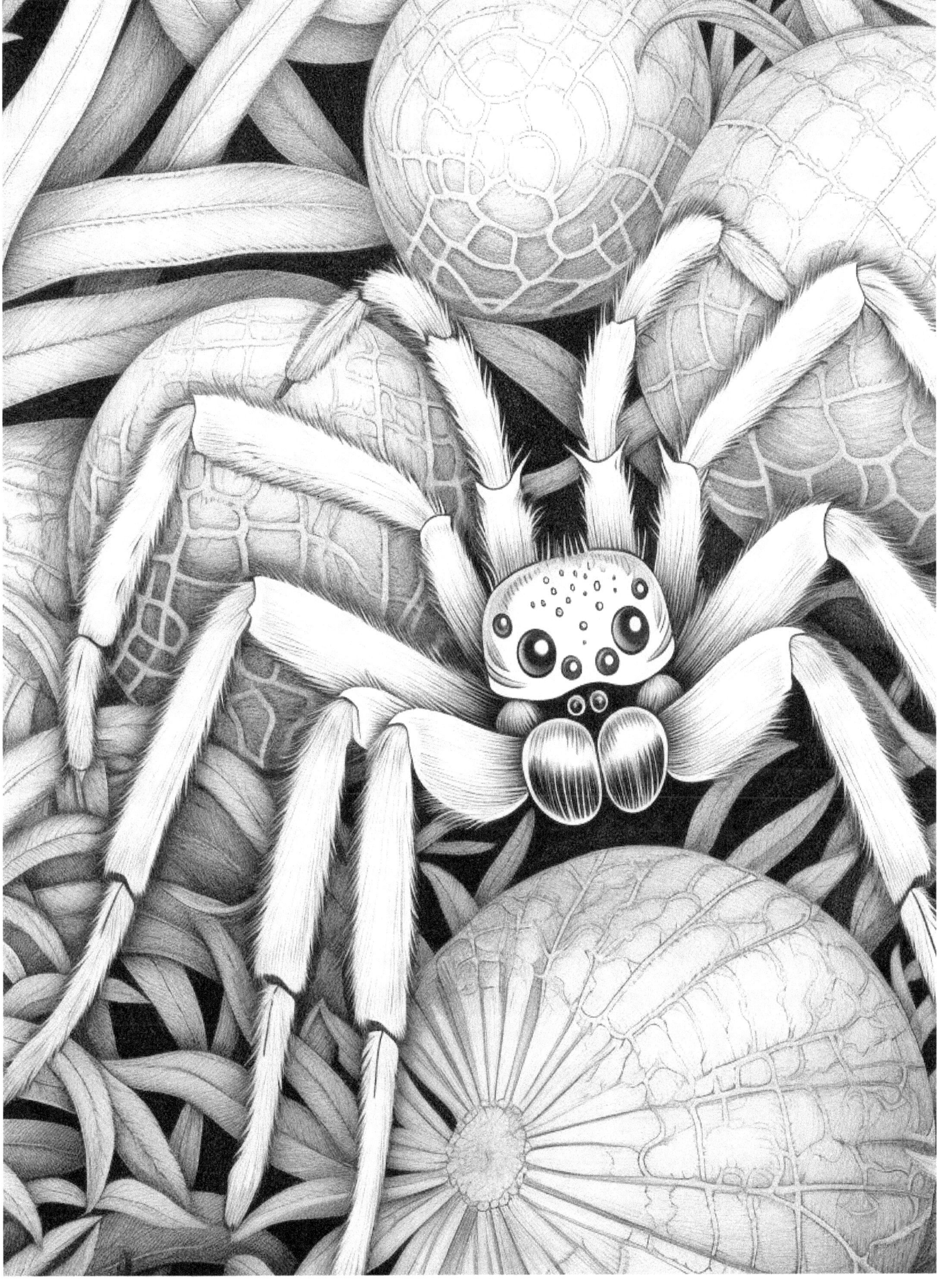

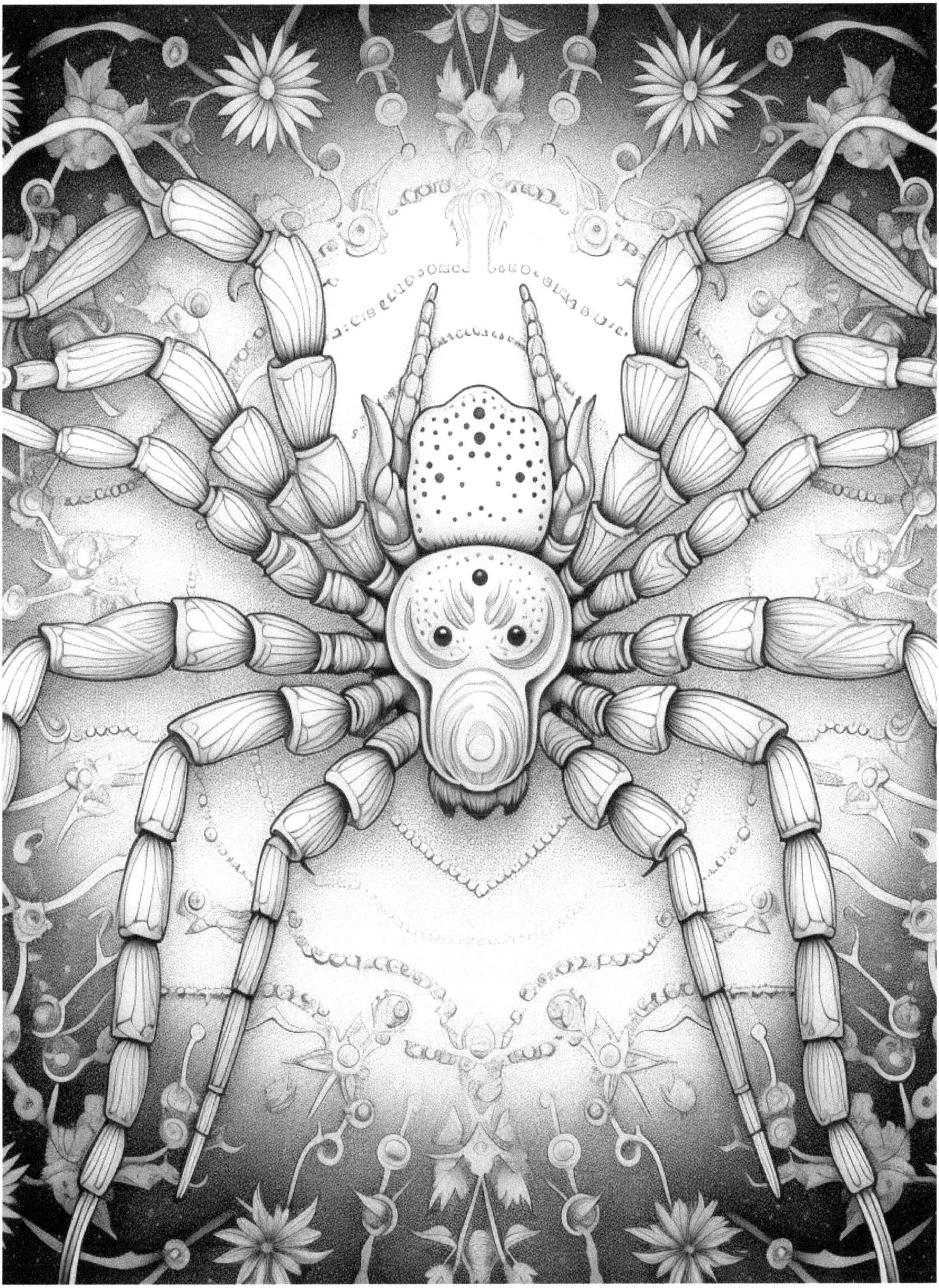

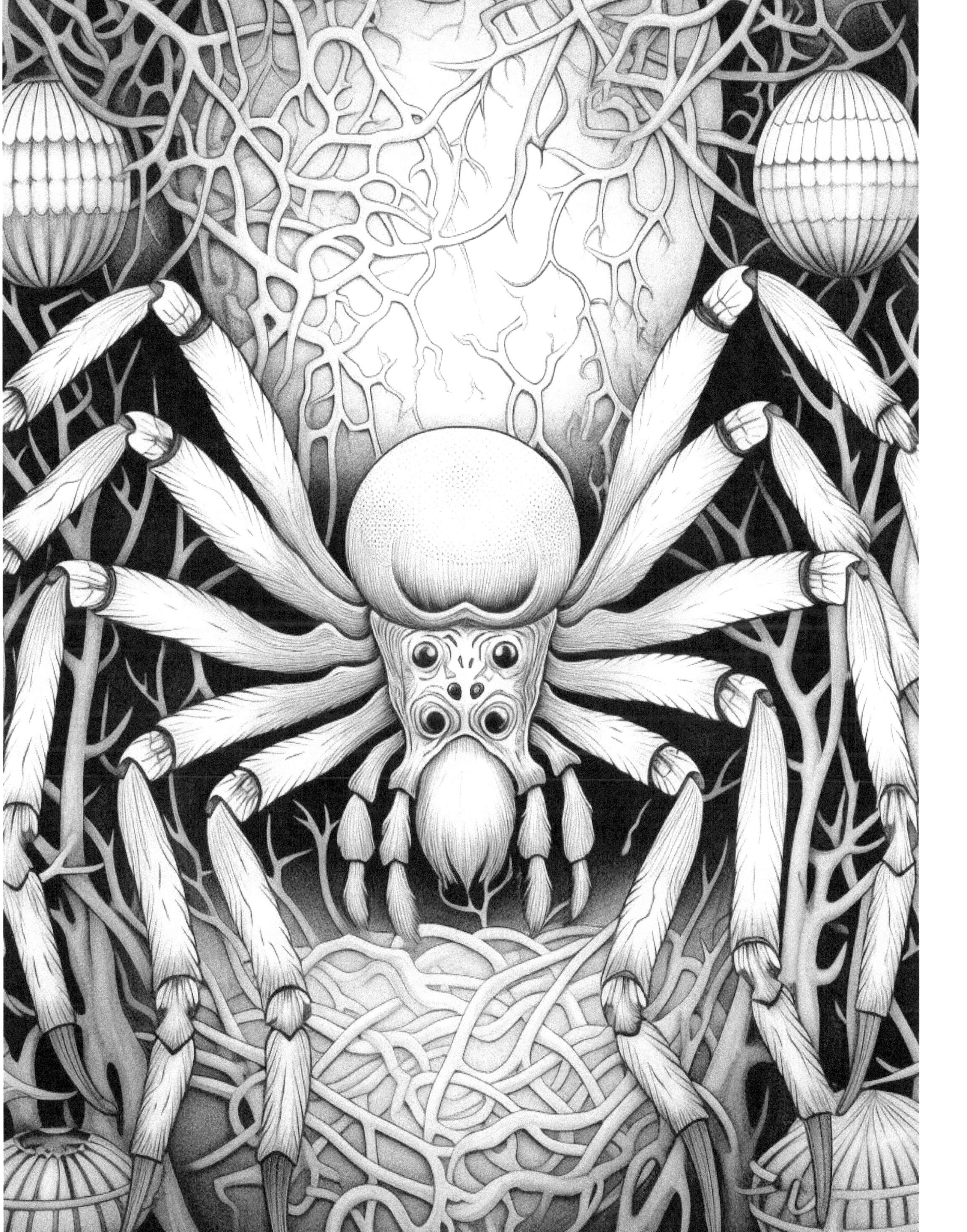

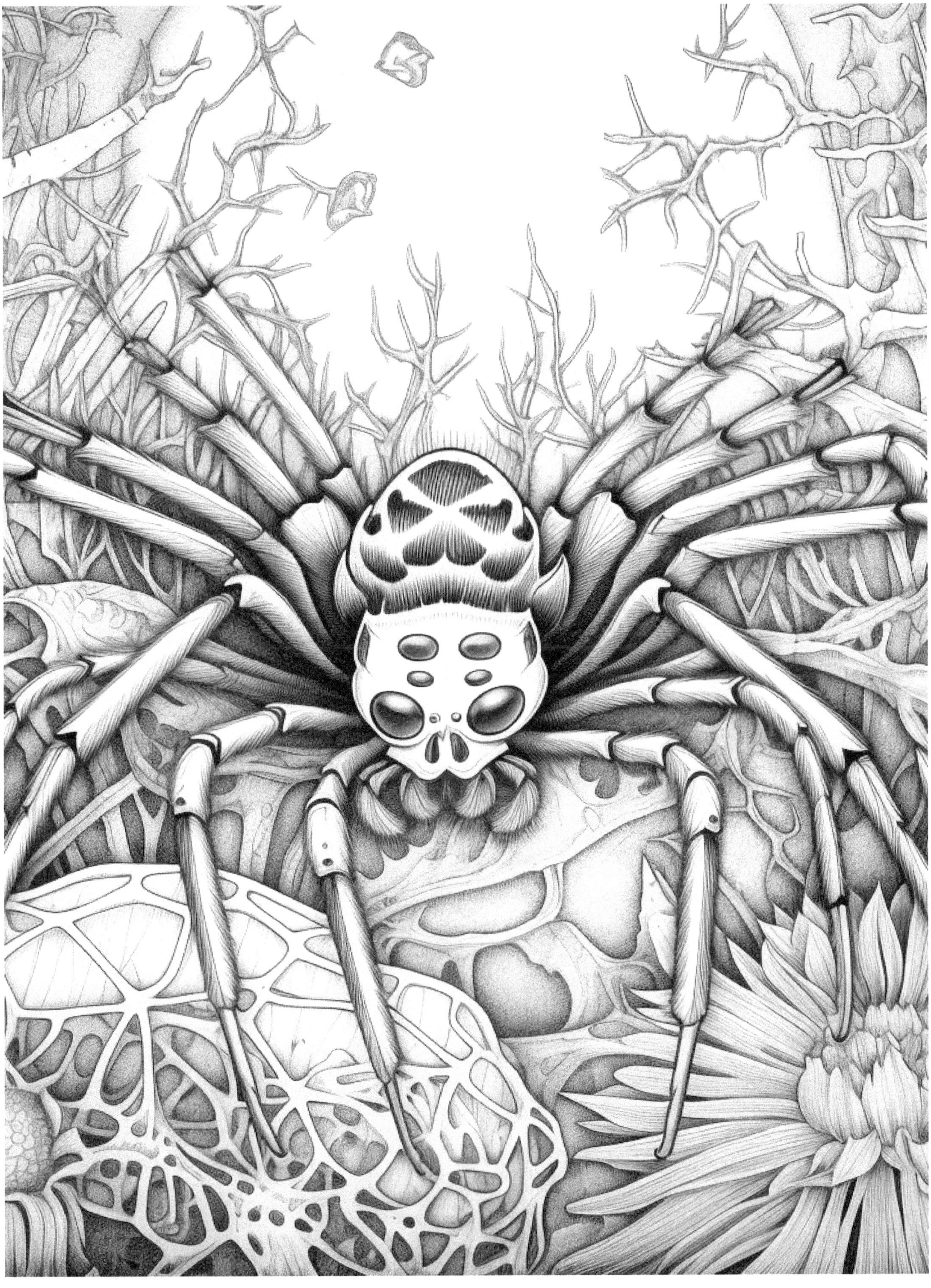

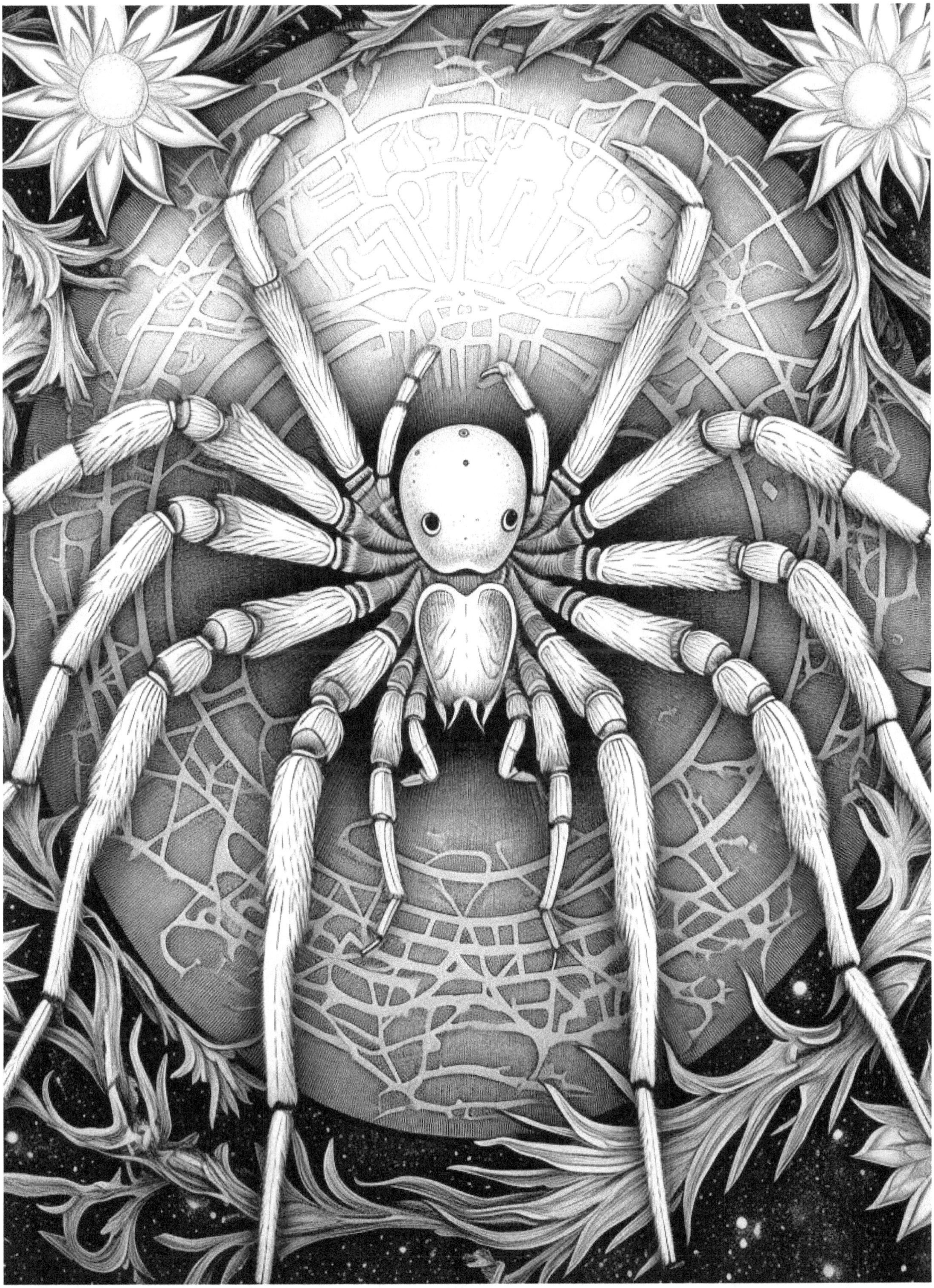

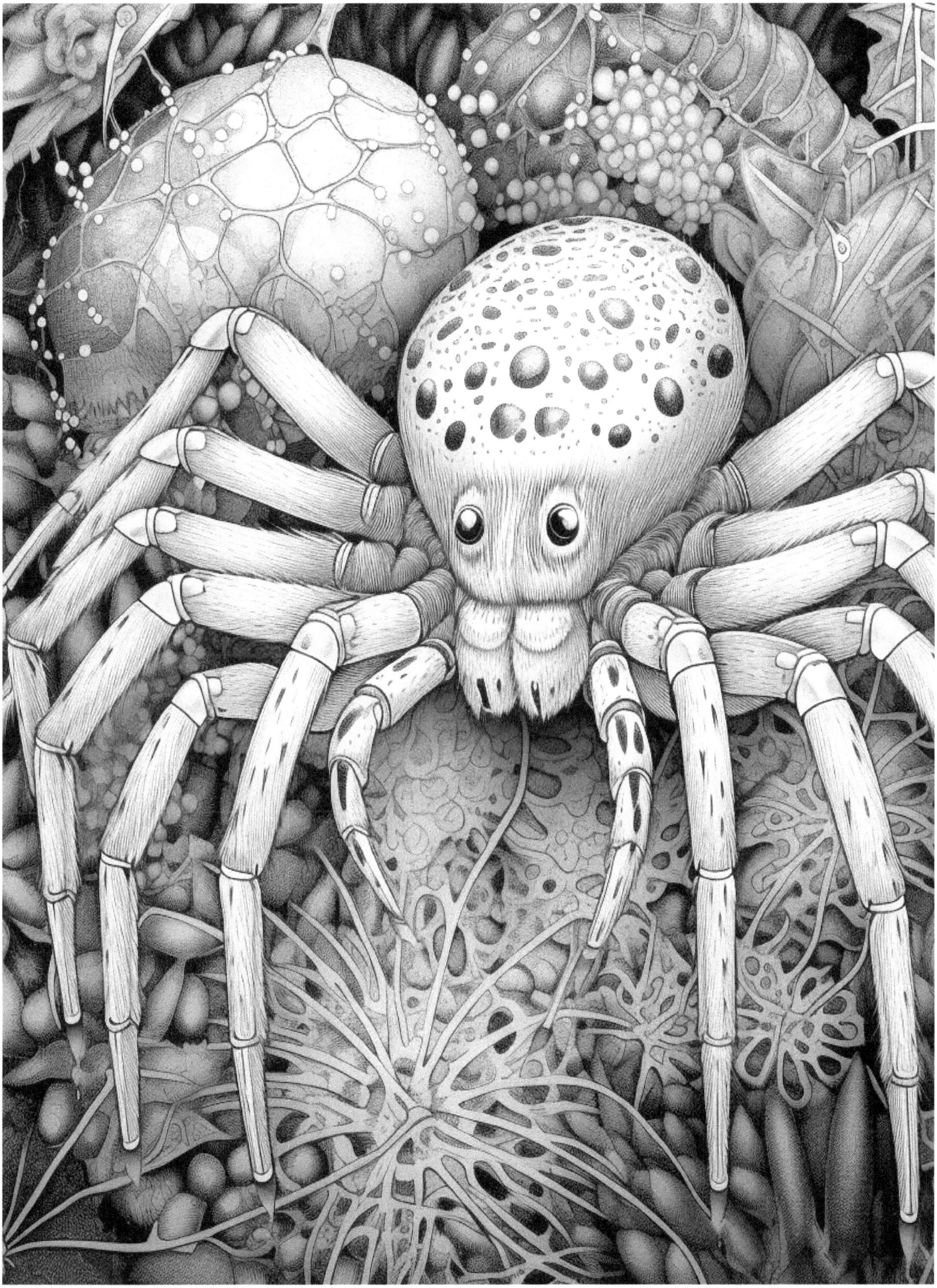

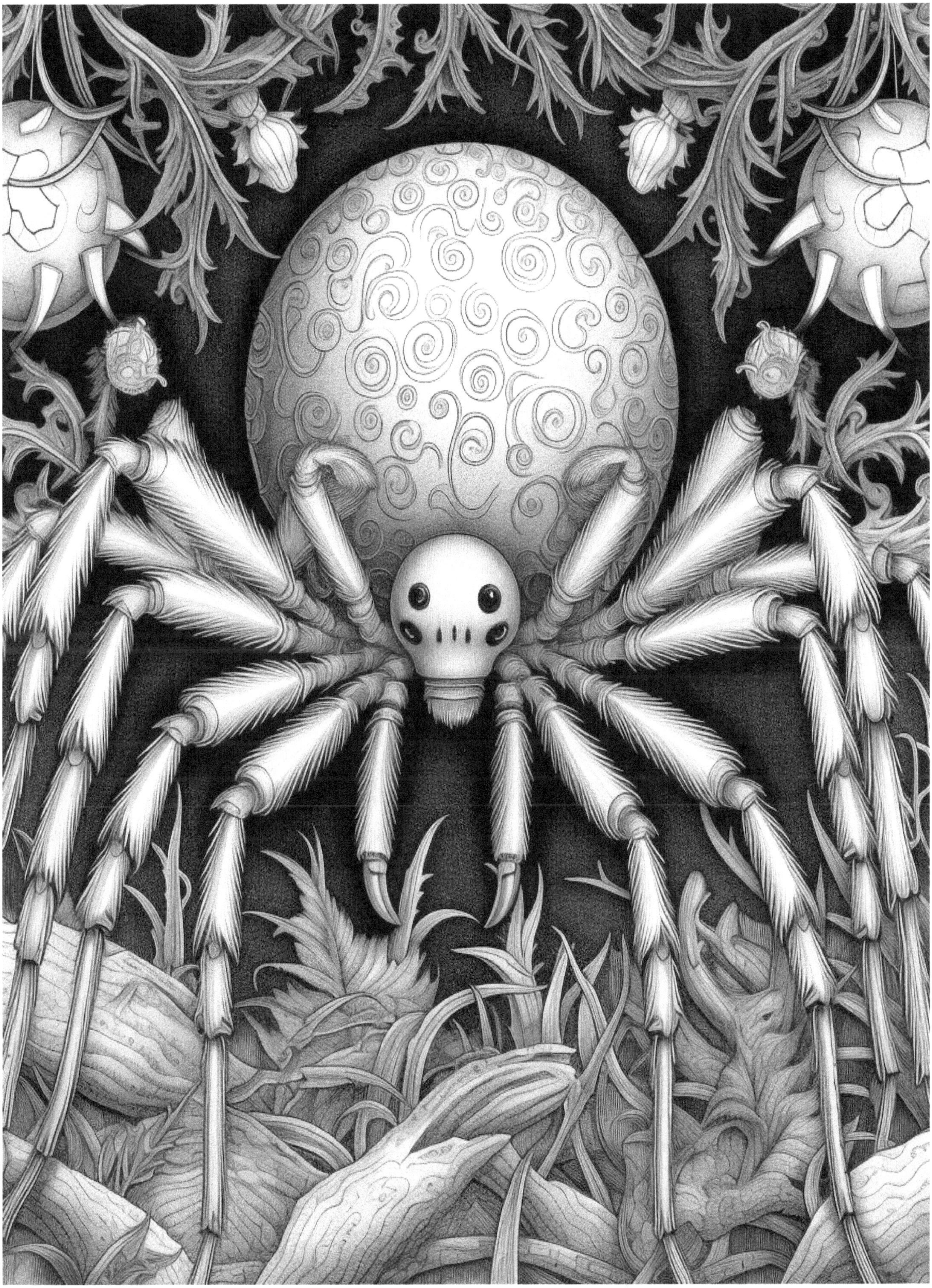

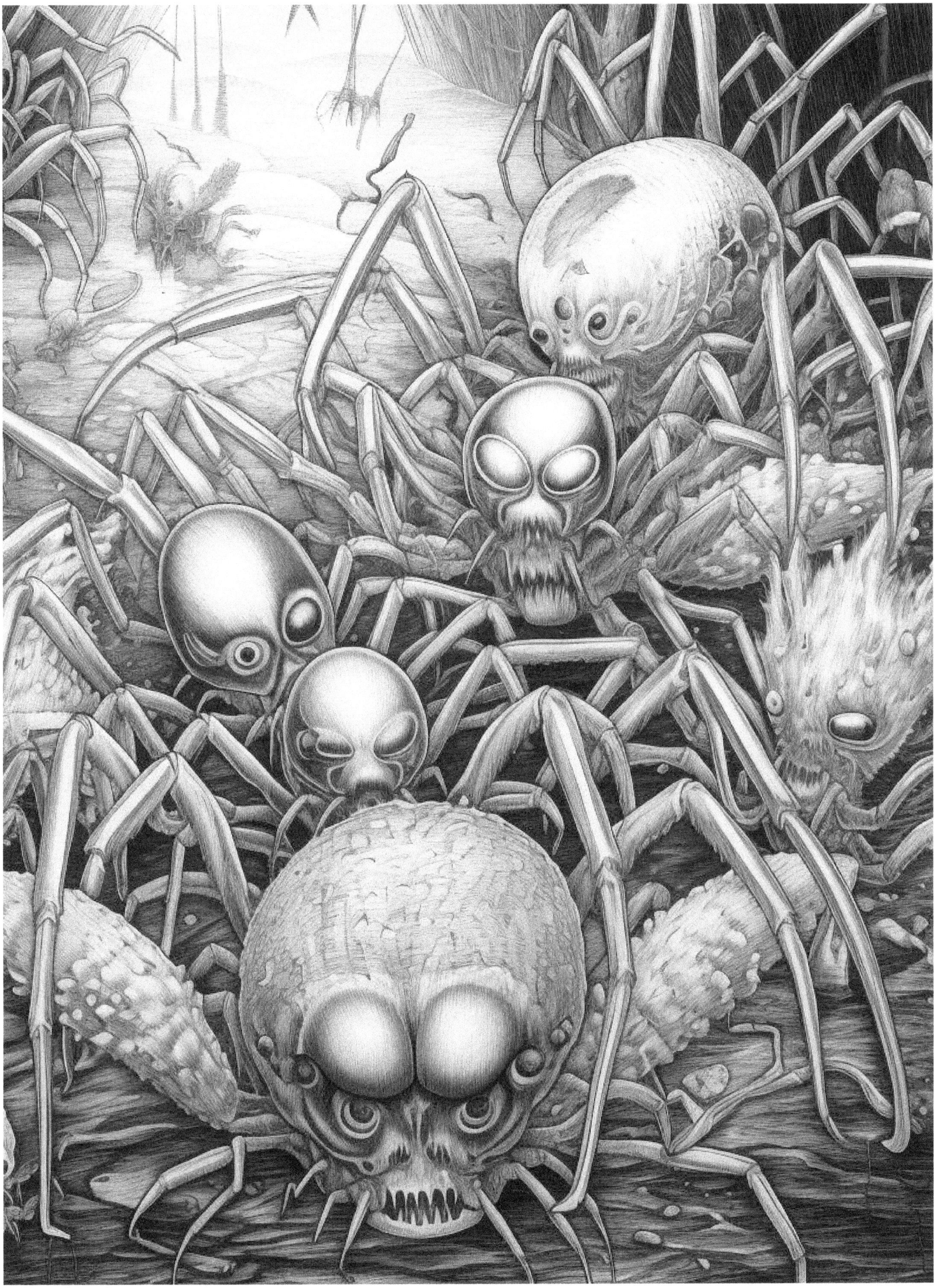

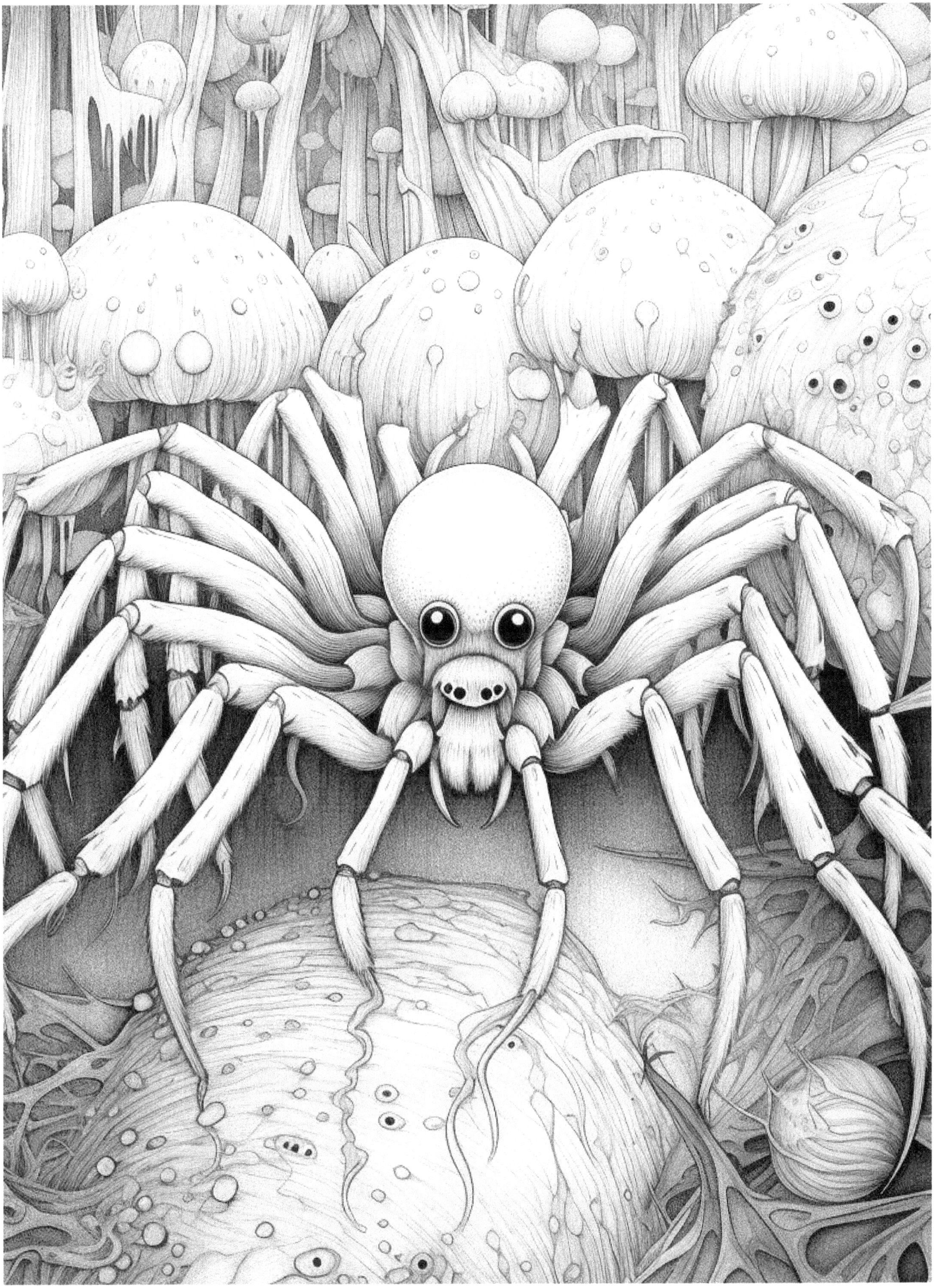

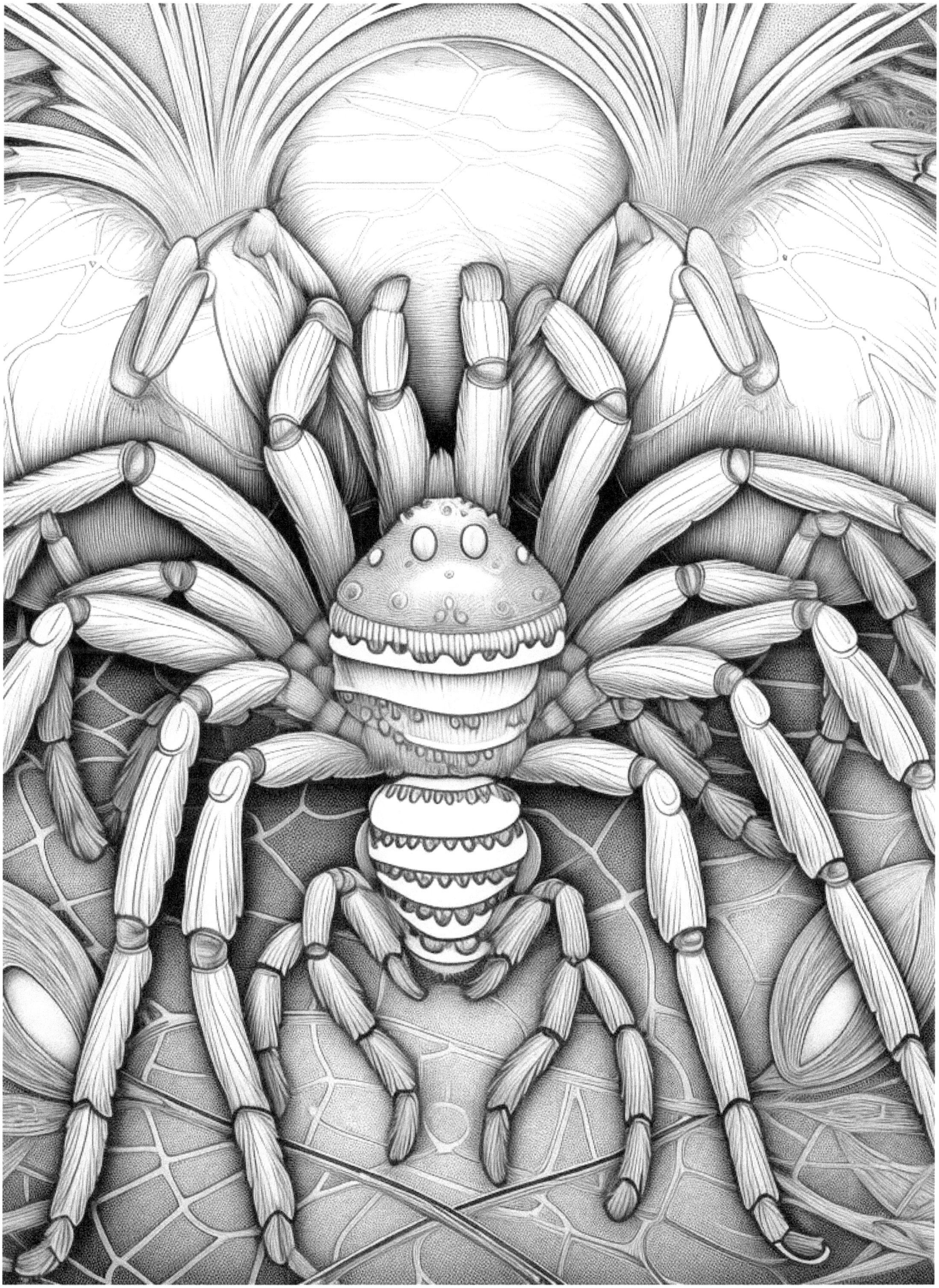

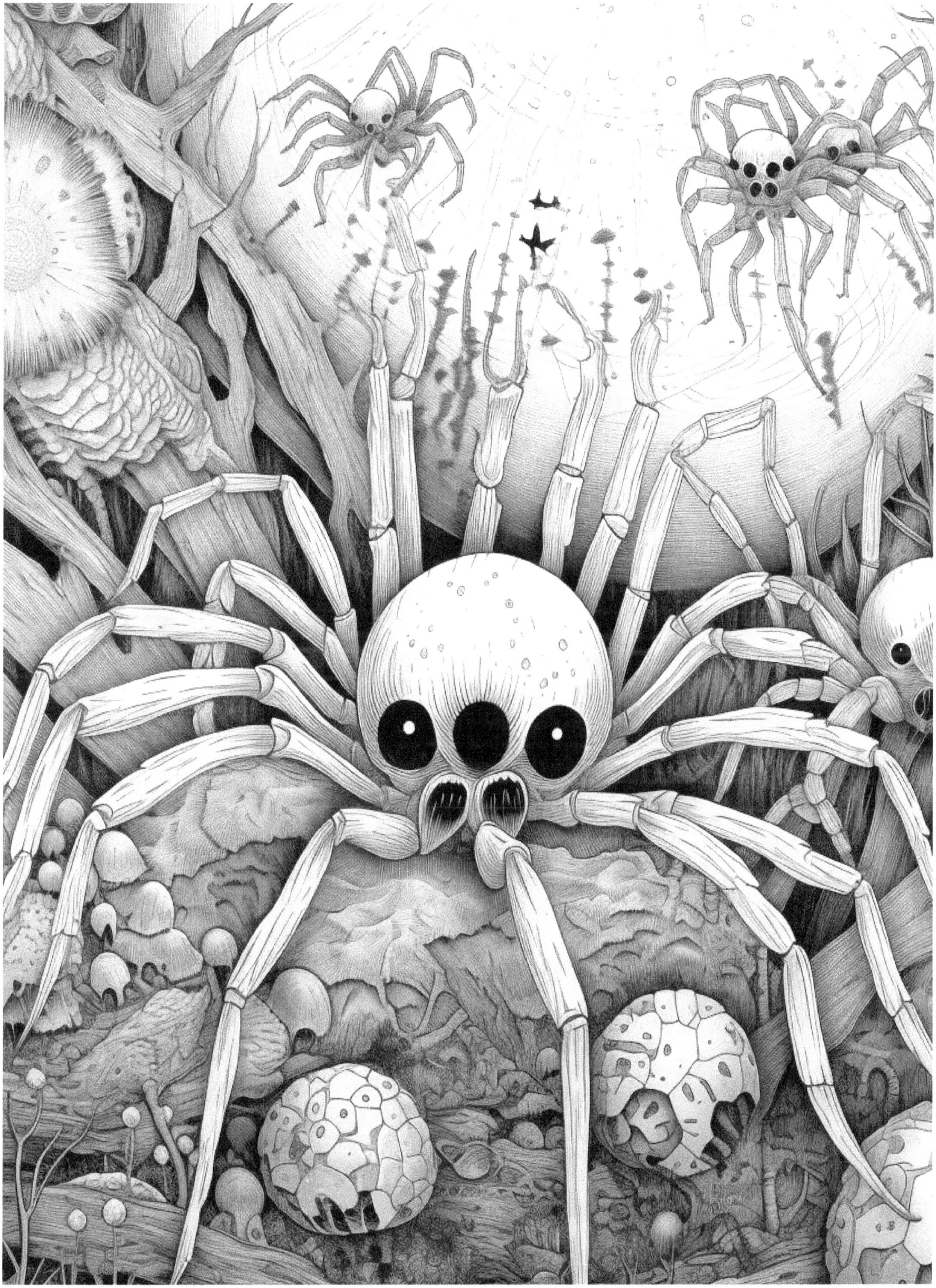

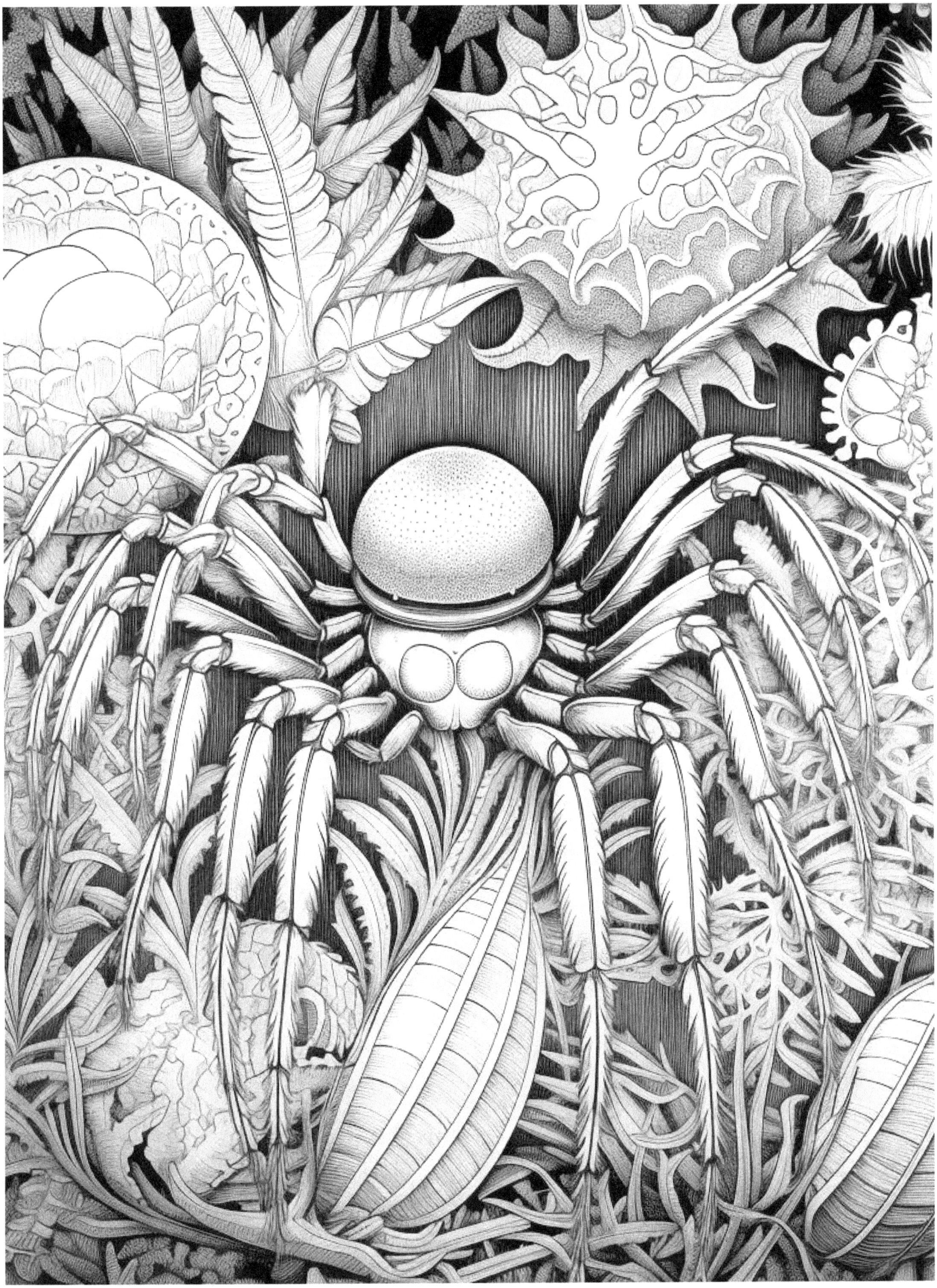

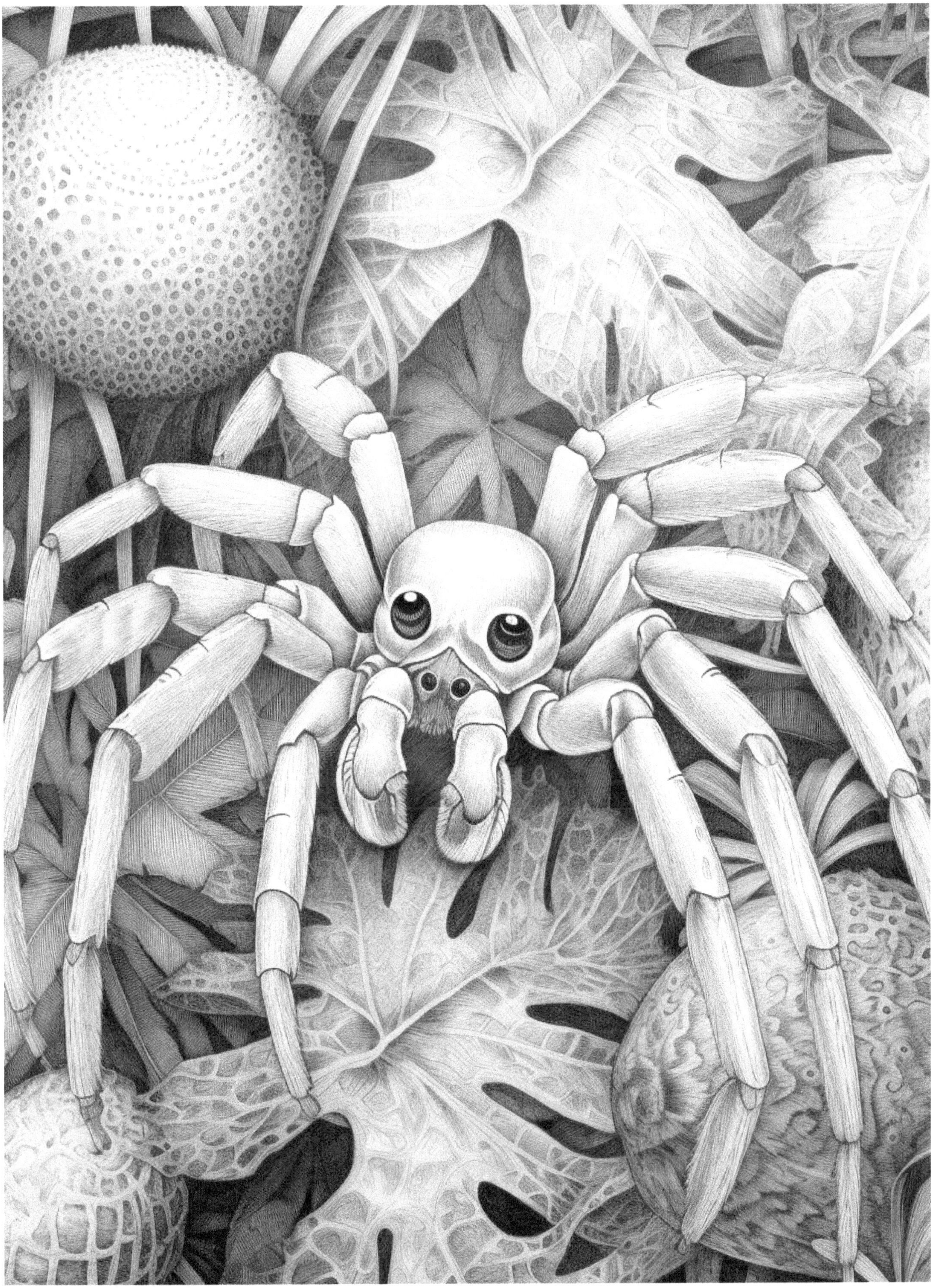

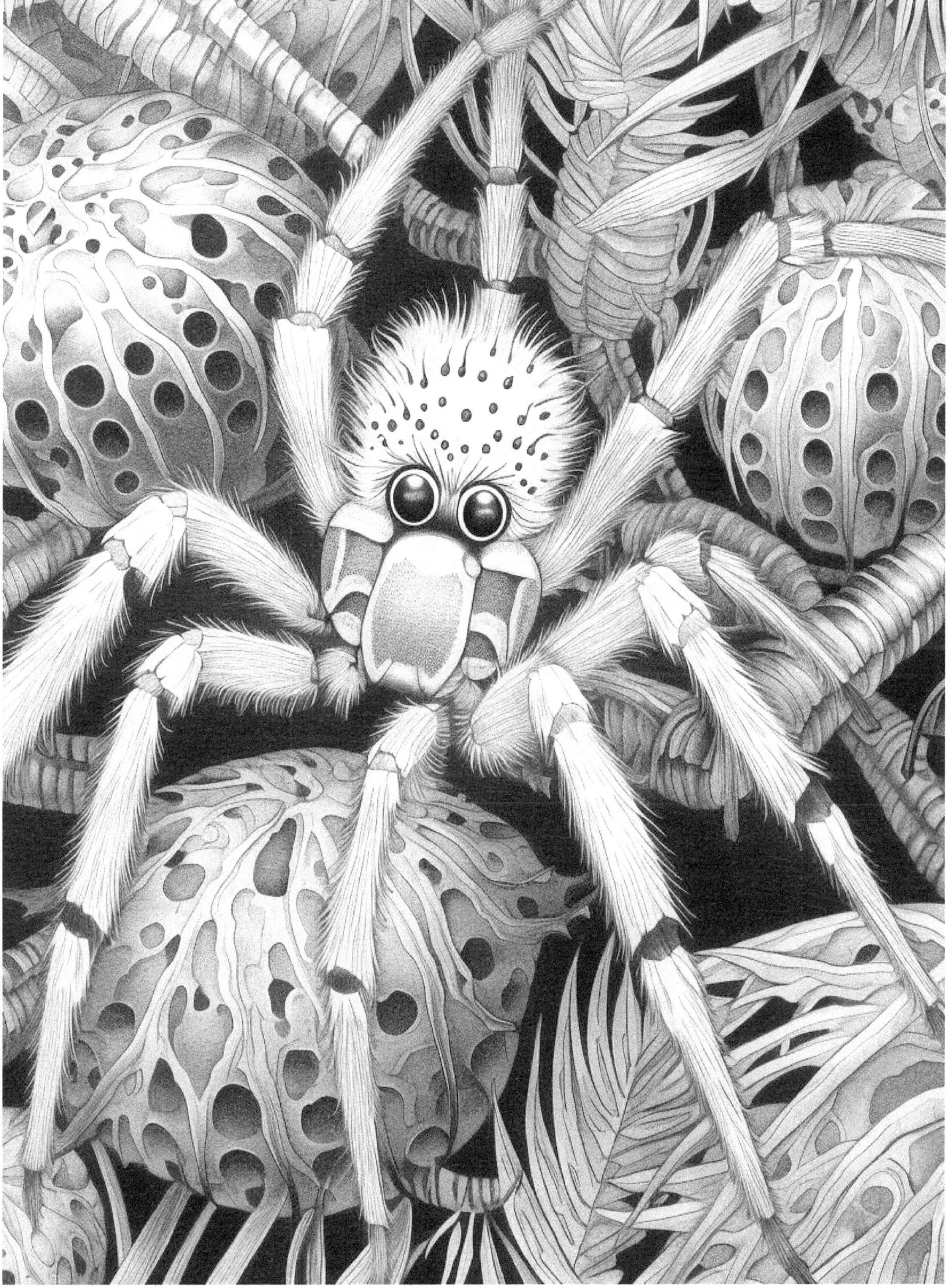

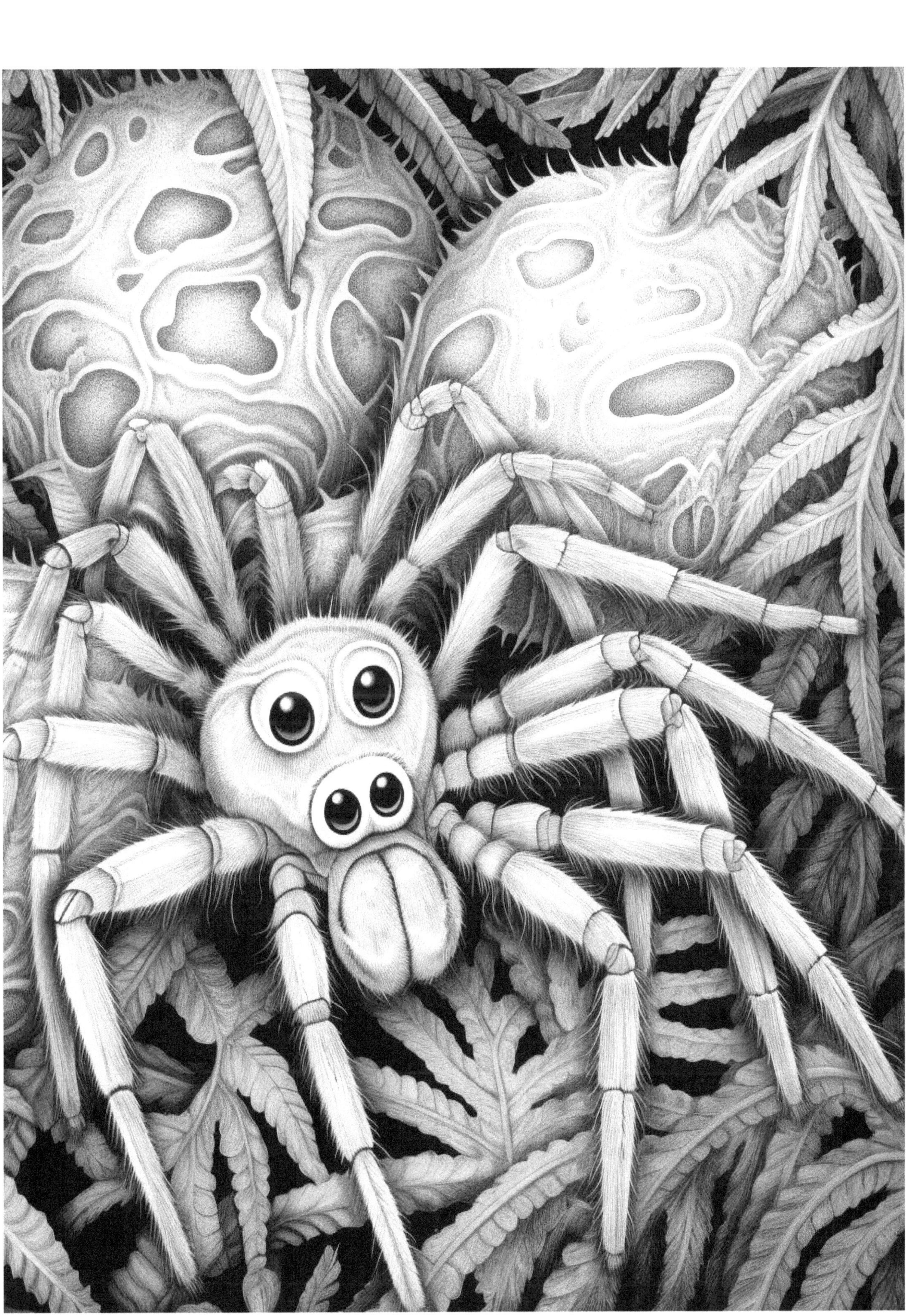

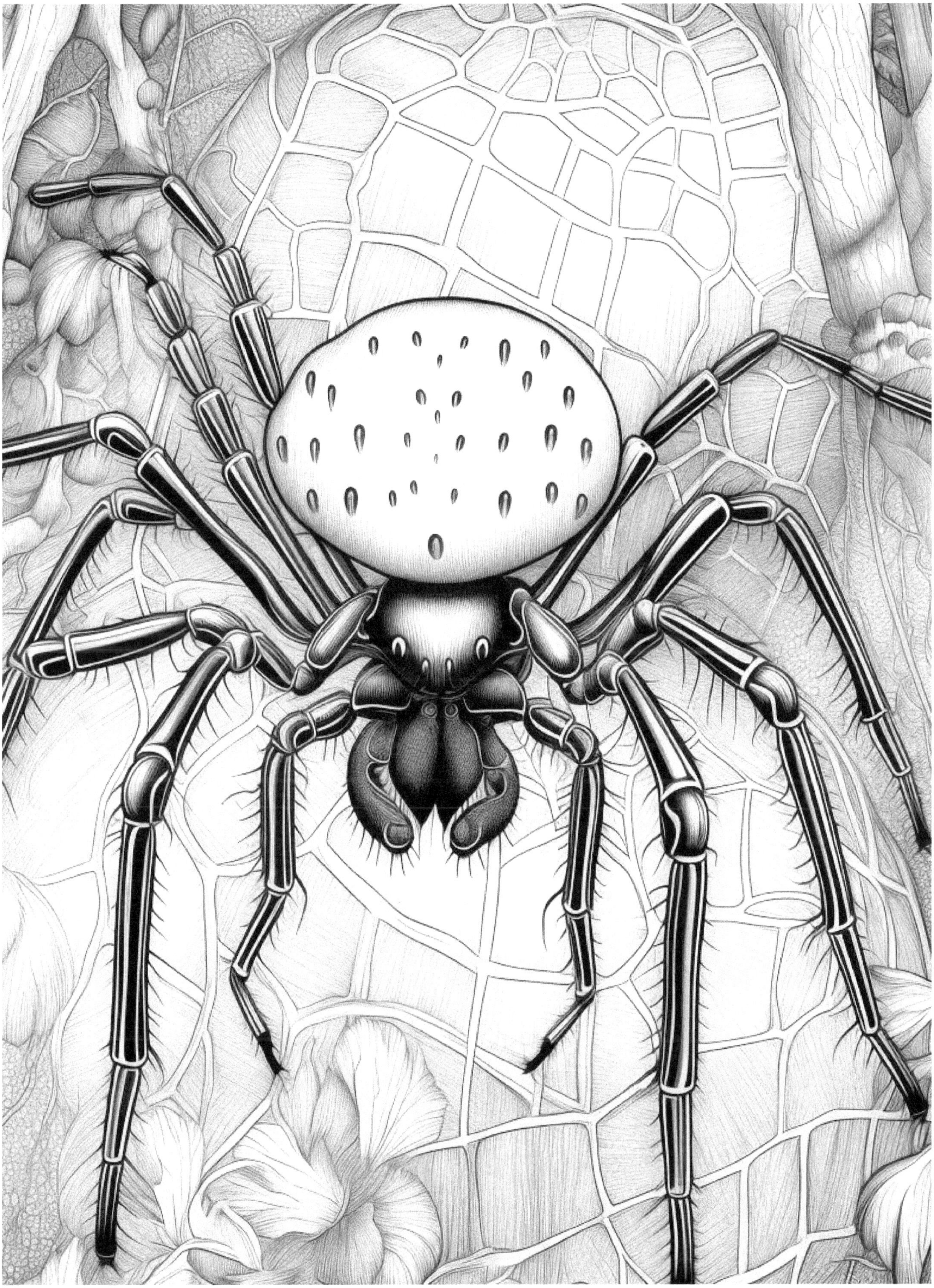

www.ingramcontent.com/pod-product-compliance
Lightning Source LLC
Chambersburg PA
CBHW080621220526
45466CB00010B/3421
* 9 7 9 8 3 9 4 3 5 5 0 5 9 *